V&R

D1628809

Markus Mühling

A Theological Journey
into Narnia

An analysis of the message beneath the text of
"The Lion, the Witch and the Wardrobe"
by C.S. Lewis

Translated by Sarah Draper

Vandenhoeck & Ruprecht

Bibliografische Information Der Deutschen Bibliothek

Die Deutsche Bibliothek verzeichnet diese Publikation in der
Deutschen Nationalbibliografie; detaillierte bibliografische Daten
sind im Internet über ‹http://dnb.ddb.de› abrufbar.

ISBN 3-525-60423-8

Umschlagabbildung: © TB und MM

© 2006, Vandenhoeck & Ruprecht GmbH & Co. KG,
Göttingen
www.v-r.de
All rights reserved. This book and all its parts are protected by
copyright. Any use except those expressly allowed legally require
the advance written permission of the publisher. Note concerning
Article 52a of the German Copyright Law: Neither this book nor
parts thereof shall be made available to the public without the
advance written permission of the publisher. This is valid also for
use in teaching and instructional situations.
Printed in Germany.
Typeset by KCS GmbH, Buchholz/Hamburg
Printed and bound by Hubert & Co., Göttingen

Printed on acid-free paper.

Contents

Foreword

A new Disney film, based on the well-known story *The Lion, the Witch and the Wardrobe*, by C.S. Lewis, was released in cinemas for Christmas 2005. It followed in the trend of other successful fantasy films such as *The Lord of the Rings* and *Harry Potter*, but was striking because the Christian message and Gospel is cleverly woven into what could be a mere fantasy story. Not surprisingly, audiences probably reached for the Narnia books after watching the film.

Unfortunately in our post-modern era, Christian teaching is no longer a standard part of the educational curriculum. As a result some children may become curious having seen the film and will turn to their parents to find out more, just as other young people might perhaps wonder about the film's background. Adults who enjoyed the film may ask themselves why it enthrals their children and what kind of values it presents. Religious education teachers and people active within the church community may use the film or books in lessons as an aid to teaching.

I have written this book for these people: it attempts to provide a clear analysis of the first Narnia story, in the context of Christian thought. The idea is not to work out precisely what C.S. Lewis had in mind, as this would be a purely historical question from which the reader would gain very little. The point is rather to clearly present the message of Christianity, show how it is portrayed in the story and to provide a thoughtful theological commentary. This book can be seen as the first steps of an adventure leading to the discovery of Christianity as the truth to be taken seriously or if one has already made this discovery, to explore deeper and further.

This journey through Narnia and western intellectual history takes place in three stages: The introduction explains who C.S. Lewis was and what the Chronicles of Narnia themselves are. This section has deliberately been kept brief. There is plenty of literature to reach for if readers wish to know more on these subjects. The main body of the book focuses chapter by chapter on the text, along with the sequence of events in the film. Each chapter is summarised, followed by a philosophical and theological analysis. I do not think I am exaggerating when I say there is much to be discovered in C.S. Lewis' story. Individual chapters of *The Lion, the Witch and the Wardrobe* can be read apart from the whole story along with the appropriate section of this commentary, however the reader will benefit more from experiencing the entire journey. From time to time there will be quotations from the text and the page numbers refer to the following version *The Lion, the Witch and the Wardrobe*, C.S. Lewis, HarperCollins Children's Books, London 2001.

Finally the postscript tackles the main theological theme – the interpretation of Jesus' crucifixion in terms of intellectual history and its models. Readers have the opportunity to embark on yet another journey to discover what relevance these philosophical and theological ideas have for our lives today.

My thanks are due to all of the people without whom this book would not have been published: In the first instance I have to mention Jörg Persch as well as Ingo Halscheidt, Akira Ueda, Frauke Hofmann, Sebastian Kuhlmann, Katrin Bosse, Michael von Seyfried, Christoph Schwöbel, Barbara Jung and Susanne B. Jung for their commitment and support, and Sarah Draper for the English translation. At last I am indebted to Tina Bruns. This book is dedicated to her.

Reformation Day,   Markus Mühling.
31 October 2005, Heidelberg

Introduction

Clive Staples Lewis, or Jack as he preferred to be called from a young age, was born in Belfast on 29 November 1898. His mother died when he was still very young and he was sent to his first boarding school at the age of eleven. Although he was brought up a Protestant he soon distanced himself from Christianity.

After graduating from Oxford Lewis stayed on to teach Philosophy at University College from 1924 to 1925. In 1925 he became fellow of Magdalene College in English Language and Literature until 1954. Between 1954 and 1963 he was professor of medieval and Renaissance Literature, this time at Cambridge University. C.S. Lewis found his way back to Christianity in around 1931 and hereafter became one of the most famous apologists for twentieth century Christianity.

Lewis lived alone for most of his life, helped by his brother Warren, who supported him in his work. Along with writers such as J.R.R. Tolkien and Charles Williams, he belonged to the literary circle known as the Inklings.

Lewis was already advanced in years when he met the divorced American writer Joy Davidman, seventeen years his junior. Nevertheless they married in 1956 as she lay on her deathbed, suffering from terminal cancer, and after she died in 1960, he took responsibility of his two stepsons' education. Lewis himself died on 22 November 1963, the same day as J.F. Kennedy was murdered.

Readers wishing to find out more about Lewis himself have an endless amount of literature to choose from, such as his biography *Surprised by Joy*, or a biography would recommend reading is entitled *C.S. Lewis: A Biography* by Walter Hoopers and Roger Greens. The film *Shadowlands* (1993), directed by Richard Attenborough, tells the story of how Lewis (Anthony Hopkins) and Davidman (Debra Winger) fell in love. The film is not completely accurate as far as minor details are concerned, but it does give a glimpse into the life of the man who wrote *The Chronicles of Narnia.*

The seven Narnia stories were published between 1950 and 1956, the first was *The Lion, the Witch and the Wardrobe,* with which we are concerned. The story is about four children who go through a wardrobe into the world of Narnia, where talking animals and mythological creatures have to endure an eternal winter under the rule of the White Witch. They long for Aslan the lion to come and save them.

In *Prince Caspian,* Peter, Susan, Edmund, and Lucy are once again called into Narnia where they must fight to help young Prince Caspian claim his throne. The next book, perhaps the nicest of all is *The Voyage of the Dawn Treader* in which Edmund, Lucy, and their cousin, Eustace, are pulled into Narnia and onto Caspian's Ship, the *Dawn Treader.* Once aboard with the Prince and the huge mouse Reepicheep, they sail to many different islands and have a great many adventures as they search for the end of the world. *The Silver Chair* tells of the disappearance of Prince Caspian's son and heir and the search to find him. After this Lewis wrote *The Horse and His Boy* (the fifth book) which is set in the same time as the first story, after Narnia is freed from the White Witch's rule, and is about a boy's journey to Narnia with his horse in the hope of finding a better life. The second to last story *The Magician's Nephew* is about how Aslan created Narnia and how the White Witch came to rule.

The last Narnia story, *The Last Battle,* tells of Narnia and England's downfall and the new life in Aslan's world. This book deals extensively with Christianity in this day in age and how it provides hope for the future. Although theological themes are dealt with to some extent in all the books, in some they are more central. The story discussed in this book and the latter two stand out.

Clearly Lewis' writing includes much more than *The Chronicles of Narnia.* As an academic he wrote many theoretical works, which we will not refer to in depth, but some of his later publications bear mentioning here. *Perelandra:* a novel, which, if anything, can be formally classified as Science-fiction, and was published as three volumes in 1938, 1943 and 1945 respectively and were the first theological Science-fiction stories of the twentieth century. *The Screwtape Letters*, his well-known fantasy story about heaven and hell was published in 1942, after which came his novel *Till we Have Faces*, published in 1956, which presents the myth of platonic love.

As a third genre, Lewis dedicated himself to presenting theological and philosophical themes in a way that can be generally understood by the average reader, the most well known of these is probably *The Four Loves*, first published in 1960 and in which Lewis describes his understanding of love as a concept, in the context of love and spirituality.

These details should suffice in giving an outline of C.S. Lewis. I recommend that those who are interested in a more in-depth overview of C.S. Lewis and his writings read the entry by Gisbert Kranz in the *Biographisch-Bibliographisch Kirchenlexicon* Volume 4 (1992), 1589–1596.

We will now begin our journey through the land of Narnia and the world of theological and philosophical ideas.

Lucy Looks into a Wardrobe/
What Lucy Found There

Sons of Adam and Daughters of Eve:
Humanity as an Organism

In these two opening chapters the children, Susan, Edmund, Lucy and Peter, investigate the house. During a game of hide and seek, Lucy, the youngest, hides in a wardrobe through which she discovers she can reach a wonderful country called Narnia. Initially she meets Mr Tumnus the faun, who invites her into his cave for tea.

Here, the terms "daughter of Eve" and "son of Adam" are used for the first time instead of the usual girls and women, boys and men. These descriptions are used throughout all the Narnia stories and sometimes cause confusion. When Mr Tumnus the faun speaks to Lucy for the first time he calls her a "daughter of Eve" and she is not quite sure what he means. In the following books these concepts are meaningless to Eustachius and the children in the experimental school because they do not know who Adam and Eve were.[1]

There is however much more behind the concepts "son of Adam" and "daughter of Eve" than just a reference to the biblical story of Adam and Eve in Genesis 2. This is because in Christianity, humanity – by which is meant all people throughout history – is not just a race or a class, but an organism: all human beings are in relationship with one another. What affects one person affects the others and no one is completely alone. Christianity therefore radically rejects individuality and any belief that states a person can stand totally alone, meaning a person can be entirely self-sufficient and autonomous. People are relational beings. Therefore we can say that what constitutes a person's value comes out of his relationships with others. This has ethical implications for actions and aspects of life affected by morality, as well as ontological implications – questions about human existence and meaning.

Nevertheless, simply the belief that all human beings are fundamentally and essentially connected, does not constitute the main idea of an organism. It is defined by all the individual parts being there for each other, whilst at the same time having different functions. Adam and Christ play important parts in this because both are seen as "beginners", as the first and second Adam (Romans 5:12–19), and therefore representatives of the whole organism: what they are and do defines the whole organism. In the same way this applies to distinctions that are applicable to people, and to sin. This can be thought of as a genetic inheritance, as Augustine said, the connections in the human organism can be taken for granted and are a result of sexual reproduction. This can also mean inheritance in the legal sense, as when one inherits possessions or even debts.

All this relates to the concepts "son of Adam" and "daughter of Eve" which we will come back to many times because it is important for the humans' exceptional position compared with the animals in the story. It is also significant because Jadis, the White Witch, does not have a place in this organism, which is why she cannot naturally (not without magic) fulfil her self-ordained role – the role of ruling over people and animals – because she does not belong in the network of relationships.

Sin as Ignorance

When Lucy first encounters Mr Tumnus the faun, he actually has an ulterior motive. He has voluntarily placed himself in the service of the White Witch and his job is to hand over to her sons of Adam and daughters of Eve.

In fact, until meeting Lucy Mr Tumnus has not seen any humans and the book in his cupboard entitled *Is the human only a myth?* shows he may be somewhat sceptical. Mr Tumnus placed himself in the service of the White Witch unaware of the implications. When he meets Lucy he regrettably understands his role and does not hand her over, but instead helps her to escape back into her own world.

This presents a double-motif: firstly sin as the result of ignorance and secondly regret through personal experience. This indicates that often central to the Christian discussion of sin is a discourse that often seems paradoxical.

This matter also unfolds in the narrative of the following chapters. In order to discuss the doctrine of sin it is necessary to give some background of how it applies to human understanding. Perhaps because Mr Tumnus is not human, the full consequences of sin will not unfold in an example about him, but instead about Edmund, Lucy's brother.

Edmund and the Wardrobe

In this chapter, Edmund follows Lucy into the wardrobe and ultimately meets the White Witch. How the White Witch seduces Edmund, or the fall itself, is not yet presented here. However, there is a sequence of preparatory descriptions in the story that point towards sin. In this instance it is not about what causes sin, but the conditions or circumstances that make it possible to sin and how these tendencies can be observed in people. According to Lewis the conditions that can cause people to sin exist in human character as virtues and vices. The children are continuously characterised by virtues and it is significant that Edmund is described in a negative light.

Discussing character seems to be viewed as a somewhat outdated topic, as well as talking about virtues and vices. Therefore it needs to be said that the doctrine of virtue belongs to the field of ethics, i.e. understanding intentional actions.

What do we do when we do something? Or: What is an action?

Intentional action is different from our general behaviour because we carry it out with intention. Things that happen intentionally always have a clear goal: People (1) behave in such a way that, out of different possibilities, they choose goals (2) which are to be achieved. Already this shows how the concept of "doing" can be identified by two criteria – the people and the goals they pursue. In order to reach these goals people use different means (3). I would perhaps use a car or a bike to reach my goal of getting to work. The means by which I achieve my goal are not randomly selected nor necessarily do I always use the most practical means because we uphold certain rules, standards and duties (4). For example, I would not drive the wrong way down a one-way street, although this may be the most direct way of reaching my destination. All of this, the goals chosen, the appropriate means, abiding by the rules and the existence of people who do all these things intentionally, is only possible if these people also have an understanding (5) of the world and their place within it.

If I want to get to work I have to be at least vaguely familiar with my surroundings.

Therefore we have identified three further traits by which "doing" or actions are characterised. So in conclusion, there are a minimum of five characteristics, which belong to the idea of behaviour: People, goals, means, rules (including standards and duties) and people's knowledge or understanding.

Different Types of Ethics

It is interesting how these different behavioural traits represent different ethical beliefs. By ethics we mean moral principles, especially those that relate to or affirm specific forms of conduct.

A moral philosophy that is primarily goal orientated is called *Ethics of goods* and poses the question of which goals or qualities should be reached. *Duty ethics* sees rules and duties as the most significant aspects of life. *Consequentialism* asserts that the means are the most important, arguing that the consequences and any side effects are justifiable if certain means are used. The consequences of an action are therefore not the same as the goal, but consequences are the result of the means used. The outcome of an action can only be one aspect of this. If one is only concerned with the outcome one is in danger of living by the motto "the end justifies the means". If one is only concerned of the means, one will act in a very conservative reserved way and would rather neglect the action altogether in order to avoid causing even the slightest side effects. On the other hand if one only pays attention to standards, rules or duties, one can end up forgetting people's needs. *Virtue ethics* as a moral standpoint focuses primarily on the person and their attributes.

Virtues

The classical doctrines of virtue pre-date Christianity. All the ancient philosophers, for example Plato, Aristotle and Stoa discussed this differently in their writings. What are virtues? Virtues are good character traits, which influence the way people behave; they are predispositions that make it more probable for people to carry out certain actions than others.

As an example we can use the four cardinal virtues *courage, wisdom, moderation and justice.* These virtues are understood as characteristics of the "acting" person, but they also support other behavioural traits, for example, if someone is courageous or brave, they are guided by their desired goal, their emotions, and also consider the means to achieve their goal. Wisdom means the person has a well-balanced idea of what is needed for the considered action. Temperance refers to a person who is not only motivated by their emotions and desired goal, but also considers the means. Christianity adds to these virtues, for example Augustine or Thomas Aquinas, with the Christian virtues as in 1 Corinthians 13 – Faith, Love and Hope.

Whereas Protestantism expressed reservations about the teaching on virtues, many doctrines on virtue were developed in the Middle Ages. One of these presumes that virtues can be acquired through practice. Could we not become righteous before God through effort and practicing virtues? Protestantism obviously dismisses this. Although these exceptions are not unwarranted, fortunately in the latter part of the twentieth century a higher regard for virtue and characteristics has emerged. Therefore it is interesting that the idea of virtue is inextricably connected to the idea of depravity or vices in character, because if a certain virtue is not developed, or is missing, a corresponding character flaw will appear in its place. Strictly speaking virtue can be regarded as the middle between negative extremes. If bravery or courage is lacking then cowardliness or laziness, daredevilry or stubbornness will appear. If wisdom is lacking, foolishness appears. Virtues and vices are not actions themselves, but can shape or form actions and behaviour.

Back to Edmund and the Children

The children – in this chapter most of all Edmund – are identified many times throughout the story by certain personality traits, virtues and character flaws. As we readers are intuitively aware of how virtues are linked to specific behaviour, certain descriptions always pre-empt particular actions, creating excitement and suspense for the reader as the story unravels. Subconsciously we ask ourselves "what is going to happen next?"

In this chapter the way Edmund's character is described does not fill the reader with hope, "Edmund could be spiteful, and on this occasion he was spiteful" (page 33). We see here that Edmund appears to lack self-control. This is illustrated again when Edmund goes into the wardrobe and unlike Lucy just shuts the door, "forgetting what a very foolish thing this is to do" (page 35). It shows his lack of wisdom and all these personality traits together point toward something bad happening to Edmund, so when he meets the White Witch in the next chapter the reader already fears the worst and suspects he will be just as thoughtless in his dealings with her.

The next chapter focuses on the reality of sin and questions of how we can recognise sin. It is important to say at this point that the basis of a person's character is not sin, but is predisposed towards sin.

Turkish Delight

After tasting the magic Turkish delight and listening to the White Witch's promises, Edmund is drawn over to her side. This chapter provides the first high point of the story, in both the narrative and the underlying message, delivering an outstanding description of sin which stems as much from the Christian tradition as it does from first hand experience.

Does Beauty equal Goodness? The Cause of Sin

According to a well-known ancient belief held by the ancient church, as well as Christians from the medieval and classical eras: *truth*, *goodness* and *beauty* ultimately coincide. What is beautiful is also true and good. According to a belief called *Universal Platonism* or *Realism* there is a separate category of beauty that is more than just the things one comes into contact with in everyday life: if there are beautiful people and beautiful horses, then it follows that beauty itself must also exist in its own right; beauty would then be regarded as of a higher order or being than the things themselves. Because ultimately loveliness is bound up with truth and goodness, these realities form existence itself, which is therefore always good and lovely. This idea of existence itself can then be identified with God himself according to the Neo-Platonic thought and theology between circa 250 and 700 AD.

Why is this important now? It is important for our understanding of evil and the White Witch. When evil wants to assert itself and ensnare people, in this instance, Edmund, it can only succeed when it appears to be good. People cannot be seduced by evil and cruelty, but only by that which appears to be beautiful and therefore good. This is exactly what happens to Edmund. After trying the magic Turkish delight, he is sure he has never tasted anything more delicious (page 44). Evil seems so lovely and therefore good, and Edmund is deceived.

Behind this is not only the doctrine of goodness, truth and beauty belonging together, but it also has a biblical backdrop. The Turkish delight is a reminder of the fruit from the tree of knowledge, which the snake offers Eve. When she looks at the fruit it appears to be good and lovely "When the woman saw that the fruit of the tree was good for food and pleasing to the eye, and also desirable for gaining wisdom, she took some and ate it." (Genesis 3:6) Again evil is disguised as something good. Obviously there is a noticeable difference; whilst Eve is tempted and disobeys a specific law, Edmund is not yet aware, as he tastes the Turkish delight, of the fatal consequences this will cause.

Eritis sicut deus: You will be as God

There is a second idea central to how sin tempts: The snake in the Garden of Eden promises knowingly "you will become like God and know the difference between good and evil"[2]. The snake promises that the humans will become like God, which here means being able to identify good and evil. In Hebrew the verb "to identify" or "to recognise" means much more than "to know" or "knowledge", it means "to be intimately acquainted with". Therefore the snake is promising the humans they will know good and evil, they themselves will be able to decipher the difference between good and evil and this is what it is to be like God. To decide for yourself what is good and what is evil promises seemingly unlimited freedom.

The White Witch promises Edmund exactly the same, not that he will be like God, but she assures him he will become prince and later king of Narnia (page 46). This promise, as we can see later on in the book, is just what Edmund wants – to be able to decide for himself what good and evil is instead of being constantly patronised and bossed around by his brother Peter, who always does the right thing. He wants to govern over his brother and sisters, by making his own judgements about good and evil. He dreams about this in the next part of the book and everything he does is based on the hope that he will be king and can then make his own rules.

Desire and Lust, Bondage and Exclusive Attention

The Turkish delight that Edmund eats is enchanted and so anyone who once tasted it would want more and more of it and would go on eating it until they killed themselves (page 45). On the one hand this is a short, but nevertheless exact description of addiction, as we know it. An addiction awakes a need that seems as strong as needs like hunger and thirst, which one cannot control or overcome. From then on this addiction determines the way we behave, what we think and want as well as our view of the world. Edmund's case is no different. Everything he does is determined by his desire to satisfy this new hunger regardless of the cost and at the expense of everything else. He is no longer free.

There is of course a lot more to this than just a description of the mechanics of addiction. It is about the effects of evil and the way it enslaves people. The outcome is interesting. We humans – and also Edmund – have been promised that we would be free and able to decide things for ourselves, but instead the exact opposite has happened. How is this possible? This requires us to go a little further and describe the difference between concupiscence and desire. Christian theology has worked out the difference rather precisely. Augustine wrote one of the early pioneering and masterly works on it.

Desire is a deeply private and individual matter. Humans are imperfect beings who will always desire something out of their reach. We cannot help but "set our hearts upon something" as Luther expresses it.[3] Indeed desire shows that humans are relational beings who are always attached to one thing or another. There is nothing intrinsically bad about this. However, it depends on what a person desires or strives for. Desire itself is not a negative thing, but it is ambiguous: if a person desires what is right it will be love, which he is truly attached to. But if a person wants the wrong thing, it becomes sinful love or concupiscence and because this wrong thing that the human desires cannot really satisfy him, he longs for it more and more.

Naturally C.S. Lewis was familiar with these descriptions of love and even wrote a book himself about love (*The Four Loves*).[4] But why does the wrong desire mean we are no longer free? As long as a person attaches his heart to the right thing his needs will be satisfied and he will remain free. Freedom also allows him to turn away from this. When this happens, he loses his freedom straight away. A need is awakened and randomly looks for something to become addicted to. At that moment he becomes dependent and his longing after the wrong thing cannot be stilled, because in this he no longer knows what is truly good. He wants to decide for himself what is good, but is blind and dependent on evil, because as soon as a person has found something to which they can direct their craving this consumes them.

Augustine expresses it as follows: before the fall it was possible for man not to sin. After the fall this was not an option, so the previous sentence is negated: It is not possible not to sin, it is impossible not to sin and this means sinning is necessary.[5]

It is obvious that Edmund is in bondage; he is addicted to the Turkish delight and therefore also to the White Witch. This lack of freedom comes across in his behaviour because everything revolves around getting more Turkish delight. He asks the Witch if he can go to her house straight away and have more Turkish delight. He forgets everything else and his sense of judgement becomes clouded as well. He defends the Witch and accuses Lucy of talking nonsense (page 52). This clearly shows how perception and awareness are controlled by the emotions.

Love and desire both present an obsession. As José Ortega y Gasset says, an obsession demands our exclusive attention.[6] This means everything we experience day-to-day requires us to make unconscious choices. When our attention is steered by emotions and desires, then effectively we are wearing "virtual" glasses because we perceive things in a new way and these glasses can either aid our perception of reality or they can be so-called "rose-tinted glasses".

Every scholar needs a desire similar to this in order to do his work and it is precisely this depth of knowledge, which sets him apart from others. He has to concentrate and focus his attention whilst hopefully enjoying the object of his research. However, when it comes to a craving or obsession, a person can go off the rails, just like Edmund.

Broken-down Relationships and Lies as Consequences of Sin

Sin ensnared man by lying and pretending to be good and one consequence of sin is that man becomes a liar himself. This happens to Edmund; the White Witch forces him to promise he will keep their meeting a secret and not tell anyone. Obviously she has to do this because those who are not yet dependent on her or infatuated by her do not have any regard for her at all and would see through the deception. Not only does Edmund intend to keep the Witch a secret, but becomes a liar himself by going against his word: he admits to Lucy that Narnia exists (page 50), but later on says the opposite to Peter and Susan to pursue his goal of getting more Turkish delight, becoming prince and later king. Edmund is in a tricky situation because he cannot simultaneously talk about Narnia and keep his promise. However, this internal conflict is not the only consequence of his sin.

A more obvious consequence is conflict between the children; the breakdown of relationships. This is not just an ethical question, but is about man's existence, his physical and living constitution. Edmund is worked up, his face is red, he snaps at the others and he is miserable. Here it is clear to see that a person is a complete entity – the things that adhere to our emotions and feelings affect us completely.[7]

Jealousy and Sin

The chapter about Turkish delight presents yet another element of sin: the connection between sin and jealousy. This does not appear in Edmund, but in the fact that the Witch is jealous and afraid of the sons of Adam and daughters of Eve. She makes a point of finding out from Edmund exactly how many brothers and sisters he has because she knows that in Cair Paravel there are four thrones and when they are occupied by the children of men, her power will be broken. Therefore she is jealous of the humans and in this lies Edmund's, and our tragedy: although he does not know it, Edmund is destined to be a prince anyway, but the Witch can still infatuate him with this promise. This is the same as in Genesis: man's destiny is to be the image of God, so the snake tempts them, saying – "you will be like God" – their destiny becomes their doom.[8]

Interestingly though, the Witch's jealousy is the reason for her plan of seduction. The humans, the four children, are destined to be kings and queens and sit in the thrones at Care Paravel. She must try and prevent this at any cost (page 28). A similar motif is found in the Christian tradition, in the writings of Augustine and Anselm of Canterbury about the fallen angels, even though this is not biblically correct.[9] It is thought that the devil is no more than one out of a few fallen angels who turned against God.[10] Why did they turn against him? Because they are jealous of humanity: the angels know that God will become man and not an angel in his son Jesus Christ, so in their jealousy they turn away and live only to cause grief for man by leading him astray. Whatever one thinks of this it is plain to see that the theme of jealousy appears in the Christian tradition as well as in the Chronicles of Narnia. Lewis names jealousy as a motivation for evil. There is, however, an important difference between the two stories: both are concerned with jealousy, but the object of their jealousy is different: the fallen angels are jealous of man because God will become incarnate as a man. C.S. Lewis does not allow for this possibility: man has a special, ruling place in creation here as well, and is also destined to be king, the same as in the bible where man is the image of God, but the object of jealousy has to be different because in Narnia, God the son is not a man, but a lion. I will go into this more later.

Back on this Side of the Door

The content of this chapter is easy to understand. Edmund and Lucy go back through the wardrobe after they meet in Narnia; Lucy tells the others about her experience and Edmund lies. This results in a conflict between the children because Peter and Susan do not know who to believe. They are seriously worried about Lucy and end up speaking about their worries to the professor and get an unexpected answer.

As this chapter is set in our world, not in Narnia, the themes dealt with are only loosely connected to the story about the fall and sin in the last chapter. Here, the focus will be on philosophical and theoretical questions of perception and knowledge.

Sin as a Disruption of Relationships and the Criteria of not Judging

The topic of sin in so far as the first affects of the children's broken relationships become clear, is evident throughout this chapter. The cause is "the meanest and most spiteful" thing Edmund could do and that is to leave Lucy in the lurch (page 51).

Although Peter believes the lie that there is no such place as Narnia and Edmund and Lucy were only playing, it does not have the effect Edmund expected. It leads to an argument with Peter because he thinks Edmund's motivation is evil (page 53).

The allegation of evil is about more than just his disposition, which was already in question before he visited Narnia. This diagnosis is based on his behaviour and the physical effects of sin. It is interesting that one consequence of sin is that the children's relationships are affected (Peter and Lucy) even though they have not all come into contact with the Witch or evil.

This shows that sin generally, in Christian understanding, is not an individual matter. Even where there is no conscious sin, the consequences of sin become visible. The children are perplexed by this new argument they are involved in. Susan understands that arguing does not make things better (page 53), but they cannot see a way out. This is why they turn to the professor, who, after a philosophical debate, offers one suggestion in light of their disagreement; "We might all try minding our own business" (page 58). Through this he challenges the children not to judge Lucy. It is not their place to judge, just as an individual cannot be judge over the sinfulness or ethical stance of his fellow human beings. Jesus' challenge is reflected here "Do not judge others, that you will also not be judged" (Matthew 7:1, Luke 6:37), as Paul also urges in 1 Corinthians 4:5.

The Law of the Excluded Third

Now we come to the content of the debate between the children and the professor. The professor asks why it cannot be true that Lucy got into another world through the wardrobe, which surprises the children because they are convinced that Lucy's story cannot be true. Here the children seem much less open and more "grown up" than the professor. They, and most of all Peter, are affected by their ontological assumptions, about the nature of reality.[11] The professor challenges these assumptions that are not supported by anything out of their actual experience, with a logical argument. He uses the so-called principle of the excluded third.[12] In general, logic argues with two truth-values, true and false. There is no middle ground possible. Statements are either true or false. In an uncertain situation, one tries to establish an alternative and to look at all the possibilities.

In this situation it is easy: 1. Lucy is lying, 2. She is crazy or 3. Edmund is lying. The professor asks the children who normally tells the truth and finds out that Lucy is known for her integrity. This rules out the first possibility and leaves us with possibility two and three. As Lucy shows no signs of madness that rules out the second option, whereby the professor suggests they consider possibility number three that Edmund is lying by denying the existence of Narnia. This third option represents a denial of Lucy's statement about the existence of Narnia. The professor suggests they provisionally accept that Narnia exists. He concludes his argument by lamenting the fact that children obviously do not learn logic at school.

How do we know what we know:
A Digression into the Philosophy of Science

This argument does not convince Peter obviously. He does not discredit the three propositions or the assumptions of the professor's position. Although he has ruled out the first two possibilities, Peter cannot bring himself to agree with the last one because it would mean accepting that there is a world in the wardrobe. Peter sticks to his ontological suppositions by insisting there cannot be a world in a wardrobe. He defends this by the empirical theories that claim if this were true it could be proven by anyone at any time, which is not the case (page 56); the children have looked in the wardrobe and found nothing.

The theory of proof represents an important debate in twentieth century philosophy of science. The strongest form here is the demand for proof or verification of a theory; that is the assumption that any theory can only be taken seriously when there is positive evidence. This demand is upheld by philosophical traditions such as Neo-Positivism and "Verificationism".[13] To restate: only what is logically derivable, and based on assumptions where there is verifiable truth, can be taken seriously.

The problem with this need for verification is that it is not logically consistent in itself. The proposal that only what can be verified can be proven true cannot itself be proven empirically. This statement in itself is much more of an ontological supposition that one can, but does not have to accept.

Alongside verification is falsification as another scientific criteria. It says: a theory can only be taken seriously as long as it cannot be falsified, even though it cannot be verified. For example, if a theory makes claims about the future, which do not occur, then the theory is falsified. Nevertheless, it was a good theory until it was falsified.[14]

Even this empirical argument poses problems, because a whole host of what we class as human "sciences", like psychology, the theory of evolution or the history of ideas do not make predictions. Even though they do not stand up to scrutiny from the point of view of falsification we will accept them anyway. Why is this? It is because there are two types of statement. Firstly, statements such as "there is x" and secondly, statements such as "all x are y". An example of the first is "there are green swans". An example of the second is "all swans are white". The first is called a "statement of existence", because it is a statement about claiming the existence of something. The second is called a "general statement" because it is a statement that makes a claim about all entities of a class or a set – i.e. in our example swans.[15]

Statements about existence are not falsifiable, only verifiable. The claim "there are green swans" cannot be falsified. But it can be verified if and when someone sees a green swan. For as long as that does not happen, one cannot know and therefore cannot disagree with anyone who makes this claim. General statements on the other hand cannot be verified positively. The claim that all swans are white is not verified by the fact that one normally only sees white swans. It would be falsified if one came across a swan that is not white.

This plays a part in Lucy's claim. Lucy asserts: "Narnia exists". This statement cannot be falsified, it can only be verified. Therefore the fact that the children did not find Narnia when they looked in the wardrobe is not evidence to say that Narnia does not exist. The professor is very cautious when he suggests to the children not to see Lucy's statement as untruth because it could never be proved as such.

However Peter insists on evidence. Should not everyone be able to find Narnia in the wardrobe at any time? (page 56) The professor does not think this would prove anything. Peter tries to save himself with his ontological assumption that "what is there, is there and is always there". Peter does not know how to respond to the professor's question of whether this is true. Peter is forced to admit that it is merely an assumption.

The professor's argument may seem trivial to us. Obviously, new ideas are always emerging, old ones appear and nothing stays the same. But here is a big problem. In arguing logic, we neglect the use of time. We do not say "there is this and that at a particular time and place". Instead we say simply "there is this or that". This is important for the so-called laws of nature. We take for granted that a stone will always fall to the ground when it is thrown upwards. This is what we have always observed and conclude that something we call gravity exists. We say "there is gravity". But strictly speaking we should say "until now, at all times and in all places there has been gravity". We can assume this is certain and it is highly probable that gravity will exist tomorrow, but we cannot know it for certain because it is in no way verifiable.[16] Back to Lucy: it would be conceivable to say that Lucy speaks the truth when she says that Narnia did exist, but that it does not anymore and this is also not verifiable.

Narnia's Own Time

At this point Susan joins in the conversation with another point of view. Lucy described Narnia in much detail but she could not have experienced everything she explained in such a short time. The professor responds by saying that it would not surprise him at all if a different world had a different time (page 57).

Following Einstein's Theory of Relativity it is not convincing these days to think that there are other worlds and other time zones. Nevertheless, we accept these ideas when we meet them in science-fiction films and literature. If one would be satisfied with this idea, one would be too unassuming.

Here C.S. Lewis is not referring to the Theory of Relativity. Therefore we do not need to explain it, which could incidentally be done very easily using school mathematics.[17] The deciding factor in the professor's argument, that other worlds could have different time scales, becomes clear if one asks what time is for; if one asks what is the purpose of time and what do we gain from it? The answer is easy.

Time makes it possible for there to be different things, for example the fact that I am not the same as the reader. Time makes it possible for unique events and happenings in the world. This is not due to time itself, but instead due to the logical structure of time. This structure has three simple characteristics, which we encounter on a daily basis, but they are so familiar that it is difficult to identify them.

For this we need to invent some descriptions. Time is first of all "irreflexive", which means 2005 would never come after 2005 because "come after ..." a chronological expression, cannot refer to itself. It would be different with other "reflexive" descriptions like: I can see myself in the mirror. The second characteristic is called "asymmetry": 2005 always comes after 2004, but 2004 never comes after 2005. Finally the third characteristic is called "transitivity": "if 2006 comes after 2005 and 2005 comes after 2004, then 2006 is always after 2004."

These three criteria are important for time. They are essential in the discussion about other times and other worlds. We imagine them to be regulated by the structures and systems as well. Indeed, everyday we experience "worlds", which show these characteristics, but are not identical to time even though they are in it. Such a "world" could be the alphanumerical sorting of a dictionary: if a dictionary was not sorted in this way and did not have this sequenced order, we would not be able to find the entries and we would easily confuse them.[18] Stories in books also follow this order, otherwise we would not be able to read them.

Because we commonly work with certain systems, which have the same structure as time, it is not difficult for us to accept the professor's suggestions that nothing is more probable than different worlds having different times, even if the flow of time is faster or slower. If time in Narnia goes more quickly in comparison to our own world, one does not notice it because the order of events – Lucy goes through the wardrobe, meets Tumnus the Faun, goes into his house, eats and finally turns back – happens in the same order as it would in our world.

The Existence of Conceivable Worlds

Peter, still not convinced, asks the professor if he really believes there are other worlds "to be found everywhere" (page 57), to which the professor replies "nothing is more probable" (page 57). The professor also wonders at this point what it is that the children exactly learn in school. In the history of ideas the possibility that other worlds exist is in fact not abnormal. It expresses that this possibility is more important than what is factual, even to the point that what is possible is in fact greater than our actual experience.

We have already touched upon the philosophies of Realism and Platonism, which state that the universal is more important than the individual. A point of view, which says, "a horse itself" or "horsishness" is more important and more real than individual horses. For this view, the concept that the possibility of something is more important than the facts is an obvious thought. In this system of thought that the possible is more important than the actual is a common idea. We have already identified where this thinking belongs: in the Platonic universal thinking of the ancient world and the Middle Ages, as well as in the idealistic system of thought of the 19th century.[19]

Empiricism, for which only the immediate experience counts and Neo-Positivism (which C.S. Lewis argues against in the last chapter), dismiss this possibility. Obviously it should be noted that today's natural sciences, if they encroach on the astrophysical cosmology, reckon with the possible realisation of other worlds. Scientific philosophers such as Karl Popper explore similar ideas.[20] For Lewis it is about a self-evident idea. He was a professed Christian Platonist as is the professor in the Narnia stories. This issue should not be underestimated. It plays a yet bigger role in the other Narnia stories.

Causality and Unavailability

At this point a problem becomes evident in our Narnia story, which we have not yet discussed. Why, when Lucy and Edmund reach Narnia through the wardrobe, and the children want to check Lucy's claim can they not go through the wardrobe themselves? In various chapters of the book a clue is suggested but not explained.

In this chapter the clue is right at the end (page 60). The children go into the wardrobe to hide from the housekeeper Mrs Macready. It is raining, just like the other times the children managed to get into Narnia. Does entering Narnia therefore depend on there being rain? This conveys the idea that humans look for regularities in the world around them. Such order is implicit in the world of nature, as we have already seen even though it is more about statistical probabilities than laws set in stone or strict causality. This gives us the opportunity to ask what causality actually is.

There are two fundamental viewpoints. The philosopher David Hume exemplifies one of them.[21] He states that we talk of causation only because we observe events in sequence in the world. We observe that when an apple falls from a tree it hits the ground and as a result of something repeatedly being observed we label this cause and effect.

The philosopher Immanuel Kant is of a different opinion.[22] He is convinced that cause and effect are independent of our observations and time. It is conceivable that someone lies on a pillow for all eternity. We would then say the head is the cause of the dent in the pillow. Therefore Kant concludes that cause and effect is not dependent on our observations and experiences in the world. Rather he means to say that the idea of cause and effect exists in man before we experience and observe the world. With Kant, the idea of cause and effect is not something that we arrive at by observation but a means whereby we structure our observations.

However this may be, Kant offers a further argument against Hume. There are also conjunctions in sequences of time that we do not class as cause and effect. When we observe that shortly before the sunset, a man appears and lights the streetlamps, this is not called cause and effect. There is a connection, but the sun is not the cause of man's actions. He, as a person, could equally not have appeared.

We will leave the question open of whether or not Kant presents a good argument against Hume. In any case, our attention is brought to another way of events being connected. Events that people are involved in function differently to those where that is not the case. The conditions necessary for events involving people – actions – are the people themselves or more exactly the intention of causing an event to happen.[23] And when people and their intentions are the reason why things happen then these events, if they affect us, are not predictable. If something happens as a result of the laws of nature and we are affected by it then the results are predictable. In such a case we can rely on something happening or not happening at a certain time and place.

Is there a parallel concept in the thinking of the Narnia stories? Yes. The children get into Narnia when it is raining. However, the rain is not a condition or cause for their entry into Narnia. This becomes clear by the way it is different in the other books where entrance to Narnia is totally unpredictable. The reason for this is revealed later. There are lots of paths to Narnia, but all of them are dependent on Aslan's will, and Aslan is a person. He has the final say whether to let someone into Narnia or not. Therefore we can say that ultimately it was the will of Aslan that allowed the children to reach Narnia through the wardrobe. An understanding of this is acutely important for all religious experiences: religious experiences are not such that we can explain and predict them using reason. If I go to church at 10 o'clock on a Sunday I cannot automatically be sure I will have a religious experience.

Into The Forest

This chapter acts as a bridge. All four children manage to reach Narnia through the wardrobe. The questions in the previous chapter about the theory of knowledge are overtaken by what is happening to them in the present moment. In Narnia they are confronted by the fact that Mr Tumnus the Faun has been arrested by the White Witch, because she has found out about Lucy's visits. The children find his house destroyed and a notice warning trespassers written by the head of the White Witch's secret police, Maugrim the wolf. They discuss what they should do. Eventually the children notice a robin that seems to know something about Mr Tumnus' fate. It flies from tree to tree, waiting in between and the children think it may be guiding them. However Edmund becomes openly sceptical once again.

Sin's Cosmic Dimension

In this chapter the theme of sin comes into the foreground again as different aspects of sin are illustrated. Whilst in the previous chapter it was about the basic nature of sin, here it is about the form that it takes, how it appears and the lethal consequences of sin. Firstly we need to mention the cosmic dimension of sin. The argument about this cosmic dimension of sin states that evil is by no means limited simply to humans with their beliefs about freedom of choice and their behaviour. The consequences of sin affect not only humanity but also the natural world as illustrated by the state of affairs in Narnia.

Throughout Narnia it is always winter, but never Christmas and the inhabitants suffer under these conditions. Biblical arguments about this cosmic dimension of sin and disturbances resulting from sin can be found in many places. For example, Adam tries to blame his companion, the woman, for making him eat the fruit from the tree after he has tasted it. She holds the snake, and therefore nature, responsible (Genesis 3:13). In the biblical text the snake cannot yet be identified with Satan, instead it is a symbol of the animal kingdom and therefore nature. Whilst only here the disturbance and separation of humanity and the natural world is expressed, Paul in a well-known passage describes how the state of nature is a direct consequence of sin.

The whole of creation, although subject only to the consequences of man's sin, is waiting to be redeemed because the whole of creation is subject to sin. Paul speaks of nature's groaning and its longing to be redeemed (Romans 8:19–23). This expresses the Christian belief that nature is no longer as it was intended. Suffering and pain, eat and be eaten are not essential characteristics that belong to nature, as it was intended, but are signs that it is also subject to sin. In the case of Narnia it is clear that as long as Narnia remains under the spell of the Witch, it will be eternally winter. As soon as the spell begins to weaken, the snow starts to melt and spring comes.

The Desire for Immediate Satisfaction of Needs as a Present-Day Sin

The breakdown of the relationships as an aspect of sin in humans plays a larger part in this chapter. Here it is spelled out how the children's relationships are affected in many different ways. The following is the first example.

Whilst the children are discussing, what action they should take after finding out about Mr Tumnus' arrest, Edmund tries to disrupt their plans by trying to get them all to focus on their hunger. They are all hungry. Obviously, Edmund's hunger is of a different order. His hunger is a result of his longing for the enchanted Turkish delight.

In this instance sin is shown in two ways: the one way by Edmund's addictive behaviour, and in another way by his attempt to make them hungry and how and when etc. it will influence their decision making. Satisfying our needs is not bad per se, but humans always have freedom of choice and their quest for immediate gratification of their need even when they are hungry is bad only if this need for satisfaction is the goal.

For example, the existence of table manners. Humans do not just wolf down their food, they organise the intake of their nourishment reactively around mealtimes, otherwise they are acting in a subhuman way. In the case of our story it is not actually about satisfying hunger because there is another important goal: rescuing Mr Tumnus. However, Edmund attempts to create a conflict between the two goals: on the one hand a risky rescue attempt and on the other satisfying their hunger. In this way

Edmund, who is in the grip of sin, tries to seduce his siblings to act sinfully, albeit unsuccessfully.

Mistrust as a Sin

Edmund's mistrust shows how he is affected by evil this also shows in his relationship with Aslan, but for the moment it is primarily about mistrust. Edmund doubts that the Robin could be a dependable guide. He suggests it may want to lure them into a trap (page 69). Mistrust really is a very important form of sin.

Luther refers to the correct biblical definition of man's right relationship with God as Faith. Faith is not simply knowledge or supposition, but faith is much more about always trusting.[24] Sin appearing as the breakdown of relationships results in unbelief, or in wrong belief. Total mistrust or unbelief is unthinkable as a human being can see that a person always has to depend on or trust someone or something. By definition faith means always trusting, so this means sin as the breakdown of relationships results in mistrust and false trust. Albrecht Ritschl, a nineteenth century theologian, even defined mistrust as the basic cause of sin.[25] In this chapter we are more concerned with mistrust than false or misplaced trust and how it is relevant to sin. This is exactly what happens with Edmund. He mistrusts all of the creatures in Narnia, the Robin, the Beavers, his own brother and sisters; the Witch is the only exception.

Sin as Indecisiveness

Closely related to mistrust is the appearance of sin as indecisiveness or to use a different word, Relativism. What does this mean? In the children's debate, Edmund argues that it is impossible for them to know who is in the right: the Witch, whom he calls queen, or the Faun. The children do not and cannot know anything more specific (page 69). Impatience and doubt represent Relativism, a spiritual standpoint which claims there is either no truth or as in scepticism of the truth is so unrecognisable that our behaviour cannot be guided by the question of truth.

Of course this concept immediately has ethical consequences. The line between good and evil becomes blurred. Good and evil can only be defined, in relation to certain goals. That which serves to achieve a goal is appropriate, that which hinders achieving it is repressive. Which goal should be chosen is unclear and cannot be clearly defined. Only in the face of this situation and Edmund's apparent attempt to have his own need immediately satisfied – his hunger – does it become temptation. This temptation for instant gratification can appear as comfort when all questions about truth and values are silenced. This kind of comfort is steeped in sarcasm. Such a spiritual state be it called ambivalence or Relativism can only regard issues of good and evil with scepticism.

However, there is a real danger that such scepticism can have nihilistic tendencies. This stance is also aptly described in the Bible in Isaiah 22:13 and 1 Corinthians 15:32: 'Let us eat and drink, for tomorrow we die!' Paul quotes this saying as a negative consequence for those who do not depend upon the resurrection of Christ. There are even books in the Bible that take a sceptical stance. As seen in the book "Kohelet". In this book it is illustrated even though the ultimate consequence of sarcasm is missing. This only comes to the fore colloquially when it says; "eat and die", which means in our colloquial saying: 'Eat drink and be merry, for tomorrow we die.'

Of course, this open sarcasm is neither convincing nor seductive. In the face of the loss of values and truth, ideas about immediate gratification appear convincing (good) and seductive (beautiful). As humans, we are familiar with this as well. Thus in our days the longing for instant gratification is nothing other than what is meant by the following well-known phrase: "carpe diem" ("seize the day").

In this respect the promise of instance gratification or abundance, should be engaged with carefully because implicit in this is a relativistic attitude to life as seems to be the case with Edmund. In the case of Edmund there are some differences: Edmund uses relativistic arguments and has already made his decision, which cast doubt on what is truly good or evil. Even though Edmund himself has already made his decision before; he sees the Witch as good and only uses his scepticism as a way of trying to get the others on his side. Concealed behind Edmund's scepticism is his conviction that what his siblings see as bad is actually good. The circumstances of this case are interesting because in everyday situations, we are confused with the question whether an argument is based on scepticism or whether scepticism is used to mask other already established deeply held beliefs.

A Day with the Beavers

In this chapter the children come across a beaver that tells them for the first time about Aslan and then invites them to his house. Edmund tries to spread mistrust about the beaver and cast doubt on his intentions, but the beaver can prove his identity because he has Lucy's handkerchief, which Mr Tumnus the faun gave him. On the way to Mr Beaver's house, Edmund sees the region where he believes the Witch's castle is and again he thinks of Turkish delight and being king of Narnia.

Once in Mr and Mrs Beaver's house the children are treated to a generous meal. Without a doubt the highpoint of this chapter is the moment when Mr Beaver first mentions Aslan. Although they only hear his name, it has an effect on each of the children. Edmund feels terrified, Peter feels brave and adventurous, Susan feels as if an exquisite perfume and wonderful sounds are wafting by her and Lucy feels as if it were the beginning of the holidays.

Before we analyse this theologically, a word about C.S. Lewis' idea of Aslan. The word Aslan itself is Arabic and simply means "lion". Lewis himself indicated that he developed the Narnia stories around the idea of a lion.[26]

It goes without saying that Aslan represents Christ. However, Lewis did not set out to write an allegory, that is a story, in which the order of events, correspond one-to-one with the story of Jesus. Stylistically, however, we do find allegorical elements in Lewis' story. Lewis let himself be guided much more by the following question; if we assume there is a land like Narnia with talking animals and the like, how would the eternal logos – God the son – become flesh incarnate? How would he appear? The answer is obviously the lion Aslan who provides Lewis with a way of presenting christological beliefs.

By Christology we mean, strictly speaking, the question of how Christ as one person could be man and God, and in the broader sense, who Christ is and what this means for us as humans. If we wanted to answer this question for Lewis we would have to pull together everything he says about Aslan in all seven Narnia stories. However this is not consistent with how Lewis reveals step-by-step who Aslan is, what he means for Narnia and the children from England.

Therefore we will also go forward step-by-step and deal with these questions as they emerge in the story.

The Theory of "External Emotional Control"

The story shows that feelings are not just internal, but develop out of the interplay between our internal and external experiences, as is shown by the emotional reaction of each of the children when Aslan's name is mentioned. We are already familiar with the elements of this interplay: Firstly there is disposition, a tendency inside each of us, which determines the way we experience what happens to us. This tendency is simply a result of our particular character traits, including virtues and vices. The second element is our capacity for relationships in our personal lives and how this is demonstrated in the concepts of desire and love. We have already seen that it is inconceivable for us not to have desires or aspirations. It just depends on the focus of these. For example when Aslan appears, our human desire reaches its fulfilment and we become aware of the right thing to focus on. This is why the children react to his name with both positive and negative feelings. If our desire has the wrong focus, as in Edmund's case, it feels like a judgment which fills people instinctively with terror when Aslan's name is mentioned or he himself appears.

Furthermore, clearly, all these reactions and feelings are not just circumstantial. Emotions or sentiments are also central to being human. They govern our will and behaviour.[27] The negative consequences of Edmund's actions reveal this; but also the other children's reactions, especially Peter's, whose feelings of courage and a sense of adventure are already affecting his behaviour.

An Intrinsic Knowledge of God in Our Inner Being

How do we recognise God? This question has stirred humans throughout history and many theologians have developed many different theories. Some need explaining in order to understand what takes place in this chapter.

One theory holds that humans have an inbuilt awareness, which is distinct from externally acquired knowledge.[28] It is mostly theologians who subscribe to Platonic thought who believe in this inner awareness. This theological notion has been extant from the time of the ancient church, whose most prominent example is Augustine, to modern times where Friedrich

Schleiermacher also subscribes to this idea of inner awareness in his "Feeling of absolute Dependency" ("*Gefühl schlechthinniger Anhängigkeit*").[29]

However, external perception can appear differently – a view which is held by theologians who subscribe to Aristotelian thought, such as Thomas Aquinas. Here one starts with the external world from where conclusions are drawn about the creator from the creation, which is what happens in Aquinas' famous cosmic proofs of the existence of God.[30]

Both these types of experience recognise a general rather than a specific awareness of God and are simply concerned with asserting that God exists, and perhaps one or two general attributes of God. It is not the purpose yet to explain specific characteristics of God. Only when Christ appears on the scene can God's identity, purposes and actions be understood. The general recognition of God is not just a so-called "natural theology" that happens when a person him or herself makes a step towards God and acknowledges him. This is also a form of revelation called a general one. The point arguments for the revelation make is as follows: God is so unattainable, that He has to reveal or disclose himself in order to be known or recognised.[31] This is not only so when God reveals himself in Christ, but also when he is sensed through awareness because ultimately God created man and it is impossible for man made in the image of God not to experience something of God.

The children experience this kind of general awareness of Aslan internally, not externally, as they react emotionally to Aslan each in his own way.

Law and Gospel

The important question is how general and specific revelation of God relates to each other. The Reformation referred back to Paul, specifically his letter to the Romans 1:19–21. In Romans 1:18 he writes about all people, Jews and gentiles, being subject to the wrath of God and responsible for their actions. The reason for this is that all have at least recognised God, they know what is right and wrong: the Jews because they know God's law and the gentiles because they know the law as well, just not in written form, but from creation instead. Based on this Luther developed a brilliant theory about "Law and Gospel".[32] "Law" is what God would have us do, what he expects from us. Law takes the form "you should/thou shalt". Naturally the content of this law is love, more specifically, the double commandment, to love God and your neighbour with all your heart and all your soul. This commandment is the core of the general recognition of God, which Luther knew so well.

Sure enough a person knows that he will fail at fulfilling this commandment. He can only love completely and perfectly if he is freed from sin, when God is revealed in Christ. When a person encounters Christ, he hears the gospel, which says "you will become", and the substance here is obviously also love. The law says "you should love" whilst the gospel says "do not worry, I promise you, you will love". When we understand the relationship between God's general and specific revelations, it can seem that we must first explain everything about Christ in order to have complete understanding. However in this story we are shown that is not the case.

The children experience all their emotions deep inside, although they have only heard Aslan's name. There are other aspects of the history of ideas we need to take account of in order to understand what happens here to the children.

Christ's Role in Creation

The missing parts of the case are the understanding of Christ as creator. He is not only our Saviour, the one who frees us from the bondage of sin, but God the son was not in the world for the first time as Christ. In fact, he created the world. This is set out nicely at the beginning of John's gospel, John 1:1–14, when Jesus is referred to as the "logos", "the Word" that was with God in the beginning, and is God. The word out of which God created everything.

Perhaps "logos" should not be translated. It is generally known that Goethe's *Faust* fails to do this. It will always be misunderstood if one thinks of "word" as a combination of letters. John's gospel refers to Genesis 1, the first account of the creation, which says that God created everything out of his "word".

The incarnation, Christ becoming a man, is described in John's gospel as Christ coming to his own when he comes into the world. Some people identify with this, others do not. Some identify with this in exactly the way it happens with Aslan and the children. This becomes clear in the calling of the disciples, which is described after the introduction of John's gospel. For example in John 1:49 Nathaniel recognises spontaneously when he meets Jesus, that he is the Son of God, although he had been sceptical to begin with and neither had he seen much of Jesus so that he could not actually know who this Jesus was. Nathaniel's confession and recognition shows that Jesus had always known Nathaniel in a deep way (John 1:48) because Nathaniel belongs to creation, which has its origins in Jesus himself. In the history of theology, new theories are always being developed about Christ's power and how it can directly affect people's hearts.[33]

Now we are armed and ready to discuss what is implicit in the story of the children's emotional reactions to hearing Aslan's name. This reaction is only understandable if Aslan belongs to the reality of a God who created not only Narnia, but England as well. The children sense this in one way or another, depending on where their heart lies and differently according to what is their heart's desire. In Edmund the Witch and her promises take priority in his heart. This is why Edmund's reaction is fear and terror, in contrast to the other children in whom a deep longing is awakened.

What Happened After Dinner

In this chapter the children talk with the beavers and try to come up with a plan for rescuing Mr Tumnus and they also find out more about Aslan. Suddenly they realise that Edmund has disappeared. They presume he was listening to the hopes for Aslan being on the move and fled to the White Witch, to betray the children and the animals. We will look at the many theological aspects found in the children's conversation with the beavers.

Messianic Prophecies

The Old Testament is full of proclamations promising a messiah or a messianic era. These prophecies presumably developed after the time of the exiled prophets. In order to understand this we must ask questions.[34] Palestine is situated in the fruitful crescent between Egypt and Mesopotamia. The geographical conditions in both of these regions are much more favourable than in Palestine. In Egypt and Mesopotamia there were civilised cultures that also had such a military importance that they shared supremacy over Palestine. Once in a while it would happen that this was not the case and instead a power vacuum would emerge. At times like this smaller areas grew stronger and were able to increase in importance. One such time in Israel was the rule of David and Solomon, a time to which the northern state of Israel and especially the southern state of Judah looked back on with longing. While both states longed for this past era of importance they developed a risky foreign policy, which in the end led to the downfall of the northern and then the southern state. Especially during the fall of Judah the rulers were so intoxicated by power that they lost any sense of reality. At this time many prophets arose and proclaimed a political message, the message of the doom of Yahweh's (God's) judgement and wrath. This happened and the upper class of Judah were deported to

Mesopotamia, into Babylonian exile. The Babylonian rule also came to an end and the Persians and then the Hellenic rulers followed. As Babylon fell new prophets arose and no longer spoke of vengeance, but of salvation. The messianic prophecies probably come from around this time. They promised a splendid messiah, a political liberator, who would come and take the people back to Palestine. This happened at the time of Cyros, the Persian king. Life under the Greeks was ordinary and later under the Romans, the oppression of Israel continued. The messages of salvation hopes for a messiah flourished. But in the early Jewish world the messiah was always portrayed as a political liberator, a splendid and powerful figure.

Christians see these messianic prophecies fulfilled in Jesus Christ. However something completely different happened because Jesus was not a splendid figure. He was not a political liberator and did not measure up to their hopes of being powerful. His was a different kind of power; it was the humble and seemingly modest power of love, which showed itself in the manger and the cross. In some ways this was much more than anticipated. But measured against what they had anticipated, it soon became clear that a large proportion of the Jews of that era dismissed Jesus because he clearly was not what they had hoped for.

What does all of this have to do with Narnia? In this chapter, exactly this exciting atmosphere of the hope and expectation of salvation is portrayed. Mr Beaver quotes a few "messianic promises" known in Narnia: 'Wrong will be right, when Aslan comes in sight, at the sound of his roar, sorrows will be no more, when he bares his teeth, winter meets its death, and when he shakes his mane, we shall have spring again.' (page 86). In this prophecy, not only Aslan, but the children also have a role to play, even though they do not yet know anything about it, as another prophecy says 'When Adam's flesh and Adam's bone sits at Cair Paravel in throne, the evil time will be over and done' (page 88). There is also a third. 'When two sons of Adam and two Daughters of Eve sit in those four thrones, then it will be the end not only of the White Witch's reign but of her life,' (page 89). Exactly as in Israel a splendid liberator is promised so also in Narnia. Mr Beaver is convinced that only Aslan can save Mr Tumnus and neither the children nor the animals can do anything to help. The rescue he imagines is that as soon as Aslan arrives, the White Witch will be disempowered and not even able to look Aslan in the face (page 86). Just as the early Jews were disappointed when they got a very different type of saviour, so it will be the same for the animals in Narnia. This will be explained in another chapter.

In the Footsteps of the Trinity

Of course there is much more than messianic prophecies in the children's conversation with the Beavers. Firstly, there is the question of who Aslan is. From their feelings the children anticipate that Aslan must be important, but they want to know more about his exact identity. They have not yet met him face to face, so Mr Beaver explains to them, who Aslan is. In order to understand this aspect of their conversation we must take a detour into the Christian doctrine of "the three in one" or Trinity.

In the Bible, there are many different stories – major and minor ones – and when all are connected and taken together we see a grand story emerge. If one wishes to summarise the whole of scripture, three main stories emerge. The first is the whole of the Old Testament which recounts the story of Yahweh, the God of Israel and the people. The second and third are found in the New Testament; the second is the story of Jesus, who proclaims with power and authority the coming of God's Kingdom, linking himself to the first story, by calling the God of Israel his Father. Jesus' claim to be the messiah finally takes Him to the cross and then seems to fail. However, the disciples profess that Jesus rose from the dead and when asked how they know this, they again refer to God: God Himself revealed it to them. With this the third main story begins. It is the story of God and His church, of which the account of Pentecost in the book of Acts is an example.

Christianity therefore has three main stories about God, which refer to each other; God and Israel, God in Jesus and God and the church. What is the point of these stories? They answer the key question of who God is and what his identity is.[35] This is the same burning question as the children's desire to know about Aslan's identity and it is the question that allows us to give a concrete answer to who God is.

When we talk about a person, we have to know whom we are talking about. If I say to someone, "Susan is blond with irresistible hazel-brown eyes", that does not help identify her because they will know other blond women. If I describe other characteristics such as clothes this is equally useless because theoretically there are others who have the same clothes etc. However, if I tell a story this makes a significant difference. By saying, "Susan was born in London, grew up in Warwick, studied at Cambridge and went travelling in summer 2003", I am talking about events specific to this person. We can identify Susan.

Conversely, such descriptions can be shortened by giving them names.[36] This is exactly what happens with the three grand stories of Christianity. They are shortened to the story of Father, Son and Holy Spirit. The name "Father" sums up the story of God and Israel, "Son", the story of God in Jesus Christ and "Holy Spirit", the story of those who come to believe in God.

When we use the terms "Father, Son and Holy Spirit", this has absolutely nothing to do with human fathers and sons, but it conveys all encompassing descriptions of these grand stories, which tell us who God is. When we hear a story about a person we only learn something about his or her identity, who he or she is in the actions that the story reports and who he or she really is, if this is what happens in the story. In the case of God, we can hypothesise this as follows. God is true to Himself and because He is true to Himself, He shows Himself authentically in these main stories: three in one – Father, Son and Holy Spirit. God is a fellowship or communion of three persons, who are in an unbreakable union.[37] God's work in Israel, in Jesus and in the church are always described as Father, Son and Holy Spirit working together as one, but this does not mean they are the same. If that were so, it would have made no sense for Jesus to pray, because one does not pray to oneself. What God is has to be thought of in the same way. When we talk about the identity of God we mean the three persons of the Trinity.

Here we must observe something of the Trinity working together. Whilst God the Father, in the Christian understanding, is thought of as working in the world but not being in the world, God the Son, actually goes into the world, becomes human and is therefore of the world. The Father is therefore thought of as transcendent (not of the world), but the Son is immanent (in the world), as is the Spirit. With this the Christian doctrine of the Trinity expresses that God is transcendent and is totally other to the world, whilst at the same time he is immanent and totally present in the world, finite. How can God be simultaneously finite and infinite? Does one not rule out the other? No, because infinite only seems to be the opposite of finite.

When I imagine a string of numbers, then the sequence 1, 2, 3, 4 is a finite sequence. However, the number sequence 5, 6, 7,..., etc., etc., is a never-ending, infinite sequence. Therefore it is easy to see that other infinite sequences can be formed, for example 1, 2, 3, 4, 5, 6, 7,..., etc., etc. This infinite sequence includes the finite sequence 1, 2, 3, 4 etc. The philosopher Hegel pointed out that the truly infinite must always include the finite. The consequences of this for religious practice are enormous. The doctrine of the Trinity expresses God as infinite and finite, and this is why we as finite beings can recognise him! For this reason man does not have to fall into scepticism and conclude it is impossible to know anything of the infinite.

All of these facts about how the Trinity is presented also play an important part in Mr Beaver's description of Aslan. He calls Aslan Son of the great Emperor-beyond-the-sea (page 86). Therefore, Aslan is also in relationship with a Father, as is Jesus

Christ the Son, with his Father. Aslan and his Father are unified in the same way – it is not an abstract unity, as with a monolith, but it is as concrete as the unity of the Father and Son in Christianity. Just as God is outside the world as well as in it, because He becomes man, the great Emperor-beyond-the-sea, Aslan is outside of Narnia, but Aslan is also in Narnia and the children and animals can know him.

There is however a significant difference between the picture Christianity paints of God and C.S. Lewis' representation of the relationship between Aslan and his Father. There is no third person equivalent of the Holy Spirit. The Holy Spirit is missing from all the Narnia stories. Why is this? One possible explanation would be that in C.S. Lewis' understanding of God, Christ plays the prominent role with the Father in the background and with no mention of the Holy Spirit. This would not be surprising because Eastern, Orthodox Christianity has always accused Western Christianity of "forgetting" the Spirit.[38] Lewis would simply be adhering to existing western traditions.

Another possibility would be to assume that the Narnia stories, constructed as they are, do not need a third figure because the Holy Spirit is the presence of God with the believers. If ever someone doubts and then comes back to faith, Christians describe this as the work of the Holy Spirit, just as at Pentecost the Holy Spirit caused many people from different countries to come to faith. In John's gospel it is the Holy Spirit who gives comfort in doubt and enables Christians to persevere.

Aslan takes on this role in Narnia. In all the stories he is always with the children and all the animals. He appears to them every now and then, but is always very real and physically there, comforts them, encourages them and helps them through every adventure.

This aspect of Christian teaching about God – the fact that he is transcendent but also immanent, can be found whenever Mr Beaver speaks about Aslan. The great Emperor-beyond-the-sea represents God's transcendence, other-worldliness and infinity. Aslan's arrival in Narnia represents God becoming man or the incarnation of the Son and corresponds to his immanence and presence with people. Aslan as Son of the great Emperor-beyond-the-sea clearly reflects the Christian doctrine of the Trinity.

Co-operative and Obstinate Human Actions

A third theme in this chapter makes clear how powerful sin is and how one can be freed from it. We have already seen that since the fall, even with the best intentions and strongest will, we cannot stop ourselves from sinning. Humans cannot not sin. This becomes clear in Mr Beaver's conversations in this chapter.

Right at the beginning Peter tries to come up with a plan of how they can free Mr Tumnus the faun from the Witch, to which Mr Beaver replies that this would make no sense (page 85). He says a human trying to act in his own strength, even with the best intentions would be useless. Deliverance from the bonds of sin is just as impossible for people as deliverance from the Witch's spells. Mr Beaver knows it is Aslan's job to save Mr Tumnus, not the children's (page 85).

This turns out to be right, but does not mean the children are not instrumental in his liberation. Quite the opposite, as becomes obvious in other chapters, they have a particular role to play. The same action can unfold quite differently. For example an independent rescue attempt by the children or a rescue attempt led by Aslan. It is the same with sin. If a person were to try and overcome sin on his or her own, he or she would be doomed to fail and would only fall deeper into sin. However when he or she is justified by Christ, he or she can certainly do good and act in accordance with God's purposes.[39] Taking care of the created world or overcoming violence cannot be independent achievements of man, but of man as a co-worker with God.[40]

Fear of God and God's Omnipotence

Another theme in this chapter is fear of God. The idea of fearing God is often seen as strange because we are used to picturing Him as a loving God, who seems to be a benign God. In the past, the idea of fearing God was not strange. Bernhard of Clairvaux in the Middle Ages along with Augustine splits this fear into two types of fear.[41]

The first is the servant fear, the way a servant or slave would fear his master, and the second is a childlike fear, the way a child fears its parents. With the servant-fear the prominent aspect is being frightened, whereas with childlike fear respect comes to the fore. People experience this servant-fear before they are completely forgiven and the childlike fear when they are redeemed and forgiven and are in the presence of God.

Bernhard was a mystic. He knew what it means to be feeling close to God and far from God. Luther also refers to the fear of God (without the mystical element) in his "Small Catechism", where each of the commandments is introduced, by asking "what does this mean?" and the various answers start with the set phrase "We must fear and love God ..."[42] Through this it is clear to see that fear and love are not mutually exclusive, but actually fear in the sense of respect is necessary for love. Love is not possible without respect.

Obviously we would be underplaying the idea of fear of God's justice if it were reduced to mere respect with fear taken away. God was in the world not only as a baby in a manger (or immanent), but He was and is also transcendent and therefore removed from us. However, He does not just transcend the world, but according to the Christian belief of creation God is also working in the whole world, all the time. Everywhere and in everything. Luther describes God's working this way as his "omnipotence".

Theologians argue about how this "omnipotence" should be understood.[43] Does this mean that everything that happens is God's will and for His purposes? If this were the case one should be considerably scared of God because it would mean that all catastrophes and crimes were ultimately God's work and dependent on His will. Luther could then say that God works secretly in all things and therefore death and killing could also be seen as God's will.[44] It does not have to go so far because God's "omnipotence" can be understood in the sense that God is effective in everything, but is not always the initiator. How?

We can take a situation in which three people are active. Person A lends person B a weapon, which person B shoots someone with in a room in the evening, during which person C is working in the electrical centre fixing the lights for that room. Person B is responsible for the action, person C knows nothing of what happened and person A is the perpetrator. All of them have an effect and had they not done what they did, it would not have happened in the same way.

This shows that God cannot be thought of as taking part an unknowingly, but as someone who accepts or puts up with evil. Is this His "will"? Harry Frankfurt, an analytical philosopher has observed that we use "will" or "want" in two ways.[45] In one sense "to want" can mean; to wish from the heart, or to aim at our sole purpose. On the other hand it can mean "should" because one puts up with something in order to achieve that which one truly wants in the long run. Frankfurt calls the second type "second order volitions" and this second type of want/wish allows us to consider how God works in every situation, including those that are dreadful and catastrophic.

God hazards the consequences in view of His higher purpose for example spontaneous human love or freedom. However in this model, especially in isolated cases of God putting up with "badness", that which is fundamentally good, remains unavailable to us. Also this weakens God's omnipotence by accepting only His "all-powerfulness" and not His single-handed effectiveness, and is only seen as respect.

Awe, which also includes a certain amount of fear, is not altogether unreasonable. Anyhow, when believers look to the cross they know that God is good. Rudolf Otto, a well-known twentieth century religious theorist thought the aspect of fear in attraction and respect should be a characteristic of every religion and religious experience.[46]

The Beavers touch on fear in their conversation. The children hear that Aslan is not a man at all, but a lion. Susan is astounded and asks if he is safe saying she will feel nervous about meeting a lion (page 87). Mrs Beaver's answer is confirming rather than reassuring "That you will dearie, and no mistake". Of course this answer does not calm the children at all and Lucy repeats Susan's question, to which Mrs Beaver answers more strongly "Course he isn't safe. But he's good. He's the King, I tell you" (page 87).

Assurance and Safety

Mr and Mrs Beaver are very definite that Aslan is not safe. Is this a kind of assurance? Or is it a contradiction? Christian belief does not offer just any old safety, but a particular kind of assurance or certainty that can be put to the test in our everyday lives.[47] Faith as trust is just as certain as me knowing that I can sit on the chair I am currently sitting on. I have no absolute certainty about this since I have no way of knowing whether or not someone has broken it or if it will collapse in the next few minutes.

Faith is the same. We can have assurance but not absolute safety. Faith is constantly being challenged by events and experiences in our lives. Nearly always if someone claims to have a strong faith, that is immune to all doubt and the challenges of life experiences, one can assume that a faith like this is not grounded in reality. Because the person for whom assurance is not enough and requires safety instead, can only have this at the expense of having a faith which is out of touch with reality. Then it is no longer faith, or at least not Christian faith. This is what the Beavers say to the children, that even with all faith in Aslan, they cannot be totally safe with him.

The White Witch

When talking with Mr and Mrs Beaver the children do not only find out about Aslan, but they also learn about the White Witch. Mr Beaver explains that she is descended from Adam, not from Eve however, but from Adam's first wife, Lilith who was a demon (page 88).

This is not entirely biblical. The name Lilith appears only once in Isaiah 34:14. Indeed she appears as a demon (the same role that C.S. Lewis gives her), in the Talmud, medieval writings giving an account of the Jewish oral tradition where she is portrayed as a demon, whose domain is sexual temptation.[48] Even though Lilith is not a biblical figure, by using her in the Narnia story Lewis can explain why the White Witch is not fully human.

Humans as relational beings always totally belong to the species or organism of humanity. The Witch does not. She only seems to be human because she has taken on human form (page 89). Mr Beaver uses this to warn them about all creatures that only pretend to be human (page 89). The Witch does this as a way of asserting her right to rule because this right is actually promised to humans and the Witch is terrified of the prophecy being fulfilled when four "children of man" sit on the four thrones at Cair Paravel because her power will be broken. Therefore it seems as if the Witch only has her power by fraud and not by right and we fear the worst when we hear that Edmund has gone to the White Witch to betray the children and the animals. Mr Beaver says he could tell by Edmund's eyes (page 92) – which shows that sin affects a person completely, including physically – "she'll want to use him as a decoy; as bait to catch the rest of you with" (page 93). But as we will see in another chapter the Witch is not totally unjustified in the use of her powers.

In the Witch's House

This chapter is about how Edmund hurries to the White Witch in order to betray the others. The first half describes how Edmund is internally affected – another brilliant description of sin. The second half is about Edmund's experience when he finally arrives at the Witch's house. Although in this chapter he actually betrays them, theologically there is nothing new. Therefore we can limit ourselves to summarising the contents. Most importantly the events in this chapter show how Edmund's sinful desires, steer his thoughts and lead to a wrong perception of truth.

Edmund is convinced that his siblings are not paying attention to him. But although the mention of Aslan secretly gives him a shock, his longing for the enchanted Turkish delight is so strong he ultimately believes, against his better judgement, that the Witch is not really evil. These emotions not only control his perception of the truth, but also his plans, thoughts and hopes. Edmund has already mapped out his life as king of Narnia and interestingly enough, his scheming reveals the grudge he has against his siblings and Mr and Mrs Beaver. He thinks up schemes for putting Peter in his place and decides to make laws against beavers. C.S. Lewis presents his betrayal in the light of a brotherly conflict, which reflects the story of Cain and Abel.

When Edmund finally arrives at the Witch's house, he is hit by the reality of his situation, is overcome by fear, but thinks that it is too late to turn back. In the Witch's garden Edmund discovers some of the stone statues and among them is a petrified stone lion. What Edmund does next reveals another aspect of sin and the way it is manifested as Blasphemy. This can mean speaking badly about God, or better described in this case, as attempted blasphemy. Tragically, – or perhaps one should say luckily, – Edmund, in his obsessive state, makes a mistake and does not blaspheme. He thinks the stone lion is Aslan, and feeling relieved that the Witch has already turned him into stone, his fear disappears and he gloats over the lion drawing a moustache on him with a stump of lead pencil (page 103).

The climax of his self-delusion is when he comes across Maugrim the wolf and assumes he is also made of stone. However, he has a rude awakening. Not only is the wolf real, but Edmund realises that the White Witch is anything but pleased with his attempted betrayal and curses him for coming alone. She is shocked when she learns that Aslan has arrived and is on the move in Narnia.

The Spell Begins to Break

In this chapter the children and Mr and Mrs Beaver flee from the dam because they know Edmund will betray them to the Witch. They know that Aslan is in Narnia and so make their way to him, on the one hand to find protection and on the other to warn him. In their flight they come across Father Christmas in his sleigh giving the people of Narnia their presents. He has gifts for the small party on the run as well.

Salvation, Creation and Sustaining Life

One of the theological themes touched upon in this chapter is the correlation between salvation and creation. What is this about? Salvation is about the way God works that allows us to be freed from sin. On the other hand creation is about the work of God, that shows his sustaining hand in the existence of the world. In the context of his work in creation there are two further distinguishing aspects.

Firstly the doctrine known as "Creation out of nothing", according to which God brings the world to life without prerequisites. According to this doctrine God working in the world is a necessary and *sufficient condition* for its existence.[49] This idea appears in later Narnia stories. The second aspect of the

"Creation out of nothing" is the doctrine of God's on-going work in creation, which can also be called the sustaining work of God. According to this doctrine, God's works in every event in the world, (which means everywhere and all the time), it is a *necessary but not* sufficient condition.[50] Therefore the difference between the two doctrines is in this last aspect, that God alone is responsible for the existence of the world, whilst his creations can and must be part of protecting his creation.

However it is important to understand that here it is not about saving the world, it is fulfilment or overcoming evil. This is much more about human beings and God working together to make it possible to sustain life. In connection with this Luther spoke about God's two "reigns" – two ways of God working in the world.[51] The first way includes the created world. In another we see God overcoming sin while the first way describes his sustaining activity in the created world. It is important to make clear that both of these activities of God are interdependent. God's act of salvation overcoming sin insists that the world will be preserved and people can, should and must take part in God's sustaining activity. Therefore human beings have the duty to remain involved and active in the world even when they are threatened by evil and sin.

How does the created order contribute to God's work of sustaining the universe? This chapter gives a very real answer as we are shown what the inhabitants of Narnia are doing. Mrs Beaver packs provisions for the journey, whereas the children can only think of running away (page 108) and Mr and Mrs Beaver look for a Beaver hideout where they can break their journey and spend the night (page 112). The Beavers know the Witch's power and know that there is no way they can reach Aslan before she does because she will travel much faster on her sledge (page 109). They know that nourishment and sleep will be necessary elements throughout their journey towards saving Edmund, so slowly and thoughtfully they prepare their escape thinking of what they need to do and thus share in God's sustaining work.

The Forerunner

Once the children and animals are on their way again after a nights sleep they meet Father Christmas who tells them that the Witch's power is weakening because Aslan is on the move. Father Christmas can be seen as Aslan's forerunner even though he has no direct contact with him and as such is a figure reminiscent of John the Baptist in the Bible. We will take this opportunity to say a few words about Jesus' forerunner, John the Baptist.

John the Baptist preached repentance, spoke of the imminent end of the world and the wrath of God which would destroy everything and everyone. He lived on the edge of a desert, apart from people and away from civilisation and he taught that the only way to avoid God's judgement was through repentance. He baptised people in the river Jordan as a sign of repentance. John acquired followers, who probably then followed Jesus, and we know for certain that Jesus himself was baptised by John the Baptist.

Jesus separated himself from John about the time of John's arrest and he collected his own disciples around him. His message differed somewhat from John's. Jesus taught through His work that the Kingdom of God was at hand and presented a different picture of God. Whereas John spoke of an enraged God, Jesus spoke of His Father, whose love was available to all, just as the sun shines on the righteous and unrighteous alike.

Unlike John, Jesus did not speak of the apocalypse, meaning a religious tide, which would bring judgement at the end of the world when only those who had earned God's love by converting would be able to escape. The gospels show that later there were followers of John, who competing with Jesus' disciples claimed that John was more important than Jesus because he baptised Jesus.

This aside, John was certainly Jesus' predecessor and knew himself that he had to step back when Jesus rose up (John 3:30). In prison shortly before his death John wondered whether Jesus was the one they had waited for and sent his disciples to ask Jesus and received an affirming answer. The apocryphal gospel of Nikodemus offers a lovely, theological explanation for John's seemingly pointless death, where his head was given at the request of a dancer in recognition of her performance at the king's birthday celebration. Just as John was for the living a forerunner of Jesus, in the realm of the dead he also proclaimed to those in bondage that redemption through Jesus should be expected soon.

"Charismas" – Spiritual Gifts

The similarities between John the Baptist and Father Christmas are limited to the fact that they are both forerunners and apart from this Father Christmas has no other function in the story. He brings gifts, that is he gives presents, which will enable the children to use their spiritual gifts. Therefore before we discuss the individual gifts we have to clarify exactly what is meant by the Christian term "charisma".

Paul addresses this issue in 1 Corinthians 12 when he talks about the gifts of the Holy Spirit, practiced by the believers and the church. Each gift is of equal importance. They all compliment each other because the different gifts work together as parts of a body where all parts are of equal value for the common purpose. Particular gifts that emerged in the early church, for example the gift of tongues – speaking in an unknown or unrecognisable language – Paul taught was appropriate only when someone with the gift of interpretation and explanation was also present.

If we look at these gifts we can say that charismas are the concrete, visible effects of justification and sanctification because they demonstrate the ways the Holy Spirit works in the body of Christ. Not only do these gifts enrich the person who has received them, but they are also given by God for the benefit of the community of believers. Therefore the gifts – or charismas

– as they echo the command to love your neighbour – can be seen and understood as gifts of love.[52]

Now back to our story. Father Christmas brings presents for the children and Mr and Mrs Beaver. These complement, support and call forth their unique talents and abilities, and can be seen to be pictures of the charismas. We will briefly consider the individual presents.

Peter receives a sword and shield. His ability is fighting, or rather containing evil with the sword, which means – when we apply the previously described doctrine of the two reigns – his calling is for assisting with God's work in sustaining life. If evil cannot be overcome then it must be contained so that it does not lead to a war of all against all. This shows that in a fallen world, from a Christian point of view, the use of force can actually be very effective. Christianity is not a pacifistic religion, which tolerates violence at any cost.

Susan is given a very accurate bow and arrow to be used only in her self defence. Her gift to be used in the service to others is a horn that brings help whenever it is blown (page 117). Finally Lucy is given a small dagger with which to defend herself and as her gift for others, a little bottle of life-restoring cordial, which refers to her gift of healing wounds (page 117). Clearly medicine belongs to God's sustaining activity in the world and here reflects the apostles healing ministry. This is quite separate from God's own saving work, which conquers sin, although this is expressed sometimes in identical language but physical pain can be overcome without sin being conquered. Conversely putting one's trust in the wrong things does not mean that one will be automatically struck down by physical afflictions. Both girls' weapons are given for self protection and this is not because they would not be brave and courageous, but because battles in which women take part are truly ugly.

Aslan Approaches

In this chapter Aslan's impending arrival is described from the perspective of Edmund and the Witch. The Witch sets out in her sledge with her dwarf and Edmund as prisoner, intent on following the children and arriving at the stone table before Aslan. Melting snow, a sign of the coming spring and the Witch's weakening power, slow down the journey. Along the way they meet a festive group of animals that have received presents from Father Christmas. The Witch refuses to believe that Father Christmas is in Narnia and in her anger she turns the whole group into stone. There are no new theological themes here but previous ones are developed further.

Shame as the Realisation of Sin

At the beginning of this chapter, Edmund is still caught up in his sinful state of mind and hopes that the Witch will give him more Turkish delight. Instead the dwarf – the Witch's servant – gives him dry bread and water and laughs at him (page 119).

It should be noted that this kind of disappointment is also described in the original story of the fall. Adam and Eve believed the snake's promise that eating the fruit would make them like God and able to distinguish good from evil (Genesis 3:5). After eating the fruit they become aware, but it is not as they hoped. Adam and Eve are aware, but of what? (Genesis 3:7), "The eyes of both of them were opened, and they realised that they were naked; so they sewed fig leaves together and made coverings for themselves." They realise they are naked. In the Middle East nakedness is tolerated even less than it is here in Europe. It is a total embarrassment and must be covered up straight away. This embarrassment left Adam and Eve feeling mocked, exposed, disappointed and ridiculed just as Edmund does when he gets bread and water instead of Turkish delight.

Initial Regret

Sin means to be totally self-centred and curved into one's self (incurvatio). A person who has actually been created to focus on being in relationship with and loving others focuses only on himself or herself. Therefore he or she is so completely cut off spiritually, emotionally and ontically that he or she becomes confused.

A sinful person is only concerned about himself or herself, not others. In this instance sin can be expressed in ways such as self-pity and self-regret. Edmund feels sorry for himself the whole time. Firstly when Peter and Susan do not react as he would like them to when he lies about Lucy and Narnia and secondly as he realises the Witch's agenda is anything but friendly towards him. When self-pity is replaced by true pity in a person's mind we can count this as the first symptom of regret, but even this is not enough to end sin or it's bondage although it is a positive sign that this is happening in Edmund. Just the same as Father Christmas (as Aslan's forerunner) and the coming of spring show nature's impending redemption, with Edmund this is the first sign of his future freedom. As the Witch comes across the group of animals celebrating because of Father Christmas, she turns the animals into stone and hits Edmund hard in the face. At this moment Edmund does not feel bad about his own pain, and he shows he is less self-absorbed. "And Edmund for the first time in this story felt sorry from someone beside himself. It seemed so pitiful to think of those little stone figures sitting there all the silent days and dark nights, year after year, until the moss grew on them and at last even their faces crumbled away" (page 125). Empathy itself however is not enough; it can be comforting, but does not overcome suffering. Even the cross of Jesus cannot be seen as God having empathy for humans because people's suffering cannot be taken away by sympathy, as Dorothee Sölle says.[53] So it is with Edmund, despite feeling empathic Edmund remains the Witch's captive and the animals are still stone.

A Part of that Power that wants Evil yet still manages to do Good

Christianity is not a dualistic religion. Dualistic religions acknowledge two principles, good and evil, as equally powerful. They share and fight over power and neither side will ever overcome the other. Throughout religious history there have been dualistic religions, for example the ancient Persian religion with two gods, Ahura Mazda, the god of goodness and Ahriman the god of evil.[54]

Dualistic thinking has from time to time been evident in the history of Christianity. For example in ancient church Manichaeism, influenced by ancient Persian religion.[55] However, Christianity has always dismissed these ideas as wrong and maintained that evil is subordinate to good. Even when talking about evil as a person the devil is subordinate to God. This means that God allows evil in His sustaining of the world, but guides and uses it for His own, good purposes. This idea is demonstrated by the famous Mephistopheles quotation from Goethe's *Faust*, which forms the title of this section, and often appears as a theme in the Narnia stories, twice in fact in this chapter.[56]

To start with the Witch tries to track down Mr and Mrs Beaver and the children. She sends a wolf to the Beaver's dam, which of course he finds empty and the wolf cannot track their footsteps due to new snowfall. The Witch is responsible for the snow with her eternal winter (page 121). In this instance the snow resulting from the Witch's evil intentions serves a good purpose.

Towards the end of the chapter the Witch's sledge becomes her own prison. It should be the fastest mode of transport, but because of the thaw it is exactly the opposite. The Witch's progress is getting slower and slower so she finally makes Edmund pull the sledge as it is faster (page 127). This is another example of an instrument of evil – the sledge – having the opposite effect.

Evil does not Celebrate

The Witch rants and raves about Father Christmas' presents and the animal's celebration. This theme of evil hating celebration and exuberance and trying to rationalise that it is wasteful, appears in the gospels as well. "What is the meaning of all this gluttony, this waste, this self-indulgence? Where did you get all these things?" (Page 123). At the beginning of the passion in Mark 14:3–9 a woman comes to Jesus and pours very expensive perfume, made of pure nard on Jesus' head. Some of the disciples think it is a waste: "why this waste of perfume? It could have been sold for more than a year's wages and the money given to the poor." Jesus says that the woman has done a beautiful thing for Him and the disciples will always have the poor with them, but not Him (Jesus), Mark 14:6.

There is a time for celebration and so-called "wastefulness" and it should not be rationalised or explained away. In this Narnia story it is understandable that the Witch has something against the celebrations because they are celebrating the coming of Father Christmas and the beginning of spring, so they are celebrating the eventual end of the Witch's reign.

Commitment to Faith in the Face of Threat

There is one last detail to touch upon in this chapter. How should we behave when facing danger or blackmail? Are we allowed to lie in order to protect ourselves, or are we bound to truth? As a rule, Christianity prides itself on truth. Numerous stories of martyrs, who clung valiantly to the truth in the face of danger and paid for this with death, prove this and the cases where people have strayed from the truth are seen more negatively.

After Jesus has been arrested Peter denies him three times in order to protect himself. In the end he is sad and ashamed of himself (Mark 14:72). This story shows how difficult it is to tell the truth when a person feels threatened. Our own strength is not enough for this, something that Peter has to realise. He is too weak. Without the presence of the Holy Spirit, the Spirit of truth, Peter is not able to stand by the truth.

Christianity is extremely realistic about this. It does not teach that it is always possible to stand firm in the truth – even those, who like Peter, do not manage it, are forgiven and accepted – but Christianity does not see lying in order to protect oneself as virtuous. This is not the same in other systems of thought. Bert Brecht explains in a Mr Keuner story, "Mr Keuner spoke out against the violence. The violence stood behind him and asked what he had said. Mr Keuner replied: "'I approved of the violence'. When later asked if he is spineless, he answers: 'I am spineless and therefore the violence cannot break my spine.'[57]

The subject of commitment to truth appears in this chapter when the Witch commands the celebrating animals to lie. She refuses to believe that Father Christmas brought the presents and challenges the Fox to lie (page 124). 'He has not been here! He cannot have been here! How dare you – but no. Say you have been lying and you shall even now be forgiven.' In the face of this danger it is a child who announces the truth. Spontaneously, without a lot of thought, a young squirrel shows it's commitment to truth (page 124). 'He has – he has – he has!' it squeaked, beating its little spoon on the table." The result is that the merry party are turned into stone martyrs.

Peter's first Battle

In this chapter the children finally reach the coast where they meet Aslan. When they see him the fear of God theme appears again because they realise something can stir up feelings of goodness and fear inside them at the same time. Aslan is pleased to see them. He takes Peter aside and shows him the castle of Cair Paravel where he will be king. When they hear Susan's horn Aslan lets him go. Susan is hiding in a tree after being chased by one of the Witch's wolves. Peter then kills the wolf with his sword. A second wolf runs away to inform the Witch and Aslan orders some of the swiftest creatures to follow the wolf so that Edmund can be found and rescued. Eventually at Aslan's request Peter cleans his sword and is knighted there and then by Aslan.

Christ is closer to us than we are to Ourselves

Particular themes fundamental to theology arise in this chapter. Aslan knows the children, especially Peter, without them having to introduce themselves. We come across this theme a number of times in the gospels. Jesus recognises Nathaniel in John 1:47, without ever having seen him before. This is not simply because Jesus can predict the future, but is an aspect of Christology because Jesus is God, the Son, the eternal Word through whom all things were made (John 1:1). This creator-quality is also present in the incarnation, when the Son becomes a man. Scripture makes clear that when the Son came into the world, He came to that which was His own (John 1:11), but the world did not receive Him. So we see an asymmetry and imbalance in this process of recognition. Jesus the Word knows the world as His own and therefore also knows every individual, but not the other way around. The reason the world does not recognise Jesus is sin. Not only does the world not recognise Jesus as their Lord, but human beings do not truly know themselves. Sin creates delusion and in this case shows itself as self-delusion or self-deception because humans no longer recognise sin and how serious sin is.

In this chapter Lucy begs Aslan to save Edmund. Aslan answers that everything will be done to save Edmund, but that this will be harder than anything the children have ever imagined (page 136). This is because people underestimate the power of sin. How does Aslan know?

The order of creation is such that God made the world out of love, in love and therefore for the purpose of love. Man should first and foremost love God and then his neighbour.[58] The reason for this is simple. Love is what sustains the world and humanity. Love is the principle, which ensures the world and man continue to exist. After the fall, when love was violated, man should have died, because the violation of love damages man. This does not happen because of God's faithfulness. God does not abandon His creation. But this does not do man any good because man is only aware of the fact that, he does not love nor die in himself. Therefore in terms of love and sin, man becomes confused.

He thinks of love merely as something that leads to a good life, rather than that which is necessary for life itself. On the other hand man does not recognise sin as something which destroys life, but only as something, which is disadvantageous. We have already said that the human species exists in a network of relationships where all are interdependent. When a person harms a relationship or harms another person he does not just hurt the other person, but also himself. However, because of the "separation" brought by sin people are no longer aware of this damage to self. A person only feels how other people hurt him or her and not the pain he or she causes other people.

Jesus is completely man and completely God. As God, He is the eternal Logos, the second person of the Trinity. He is and has been, in relationship with the Father and the Holy Spirit. When He becomes man and enters into the realm of humanity, He is not affected by the separation of sin and does not become deluded. This also means, as the Scottish theologian Thomas Erskine of Linlathen points out, that Jesus directly feels our pain and experiences every sinful injury caused to the human race.[59] Therefore Jesus is intellectually and emotionally aware and is closer to every person than they are to themselves.

The above provides a backdrop to the passage in this chapter where Aslan recognises and knows the children, and understands the seriousness of sin better than they do. They think it would be enough if Edmund were freed from the Witch, but Aslan knows that this would in no way suffice.

Deep Magic from the Dawn of Time

This and the two following chapters constitute the climax of the whole story, and its theological content. Firstly the story returns to the Witch. She realises there is no way she can reach the stone table by the sea before Aslan and so agrees with the dwarf that Edmund should be killed there and then. This means Edmund's death has a double meaning. On the one hand, Edmund dying would give the Witch an advantage because the prophecy says that in order for the Witch's reign to be broken sons of Adam and daughters of Eve must occupy all four thrones at Cair Paravel. She thinks killing Edmund can overcome this because then only three thrones will be filled. The Witch and the Dwarf also talk about it being necessary for Edmund to die, quite apart from their own agenda (page 143). This seems to be about a ritual function of Edmund's planned death because the stone table, that the Witch still has to reach, would be the proper place for such a sacrifice – a word used explicitly by the Witch (page 143). The Dwarf immediately makes the necessary preparations for the sacrifice.

Edmund is so exhausted as the Witch's prisoner that he no longer cares what is going on around him and does not put up a fight (page 142). Whilst she is sharpening her knife, the creatures sent by Aslan to follow the wolf arrive. The Witch is caught by surprise. They rescue Edmund and immediately take him to Aslan. The Witch and the Dwarf escape and she then decides to call upon all her followers.

After Aslan has talked with Edmund for a long time, he sends him back to the others. Edmund is full of remorse and asks for forgiveness, but Aslan recommends that there is no need for them to talk about what is past (page 147). At this point, a messenger from the Witch arrives. She requests safe conduct to come and speak with Aslan himself. He agrees and in their conversation the Witch points out that Edmund is a traitor, having betrayed Aslan and the children (page 149).

Before the dawn of time in Narnia, there was a deep magic that the Emperor put into Narnia at the very beginning and is written on the stone table (page 149). According to the law every traitor belongs to the Witch and she has the right – or rather duty – to kill for every act of treachery (page 150). If she does not the law says that all Narnia will be overturned and perish in fire and water (page 150).

Sadly the animals realise exactly how much lawful power the Witch possesses. She is the Emperor's – Aslan's father's – executioner and with this she insists that Edmund be handed over so she can kill him. Susan pleads with Aslan asking if there is nothing that can be done to work against the Deep Magic and learns from Aslan that it is impossible to do anything against the Emperor's will. Aslan and the Witch talk privately and when they are finished, he tells the children "you can all come back. I have settled the matter. She has renounced the claim on your brother's blood." Finally in this chapter the reader learns that Aslan has made a promise to the Witch, which there is no question of him keeping, even if the Witch doubts him (page 152).

Sin as Sloth

At the beginning of this chapter another aspect of the phenomenological way that sin appears is shown by Edmund's behaviour. He no longer cares about anything happening around him. This idea that sin expresses itself in sloth is a classical idea. This comes as no surprise as melancholy is also one of the seven deadly sins.[60] History refers more to sins with active components, where sin is emphasised as arrogance or hybris, but the passive components of sin were also always there in the history of theology.

The great Protestant theologian Karl Barth must be credited in the twentieth century, for having highlighted the importance of this form of sin, in his writings about sin as sloth.[61] It also becomes clear how important this is if one shows that sin always means a break or rupture of relationship, therefore leading to a distorted self-image of the sinner. A person who is slothful and resigned refuses to recognise the promise of human relationship. It is no excuse that this is not the result of a conscious decision because we have already seen that sin controls a person's emotional state, which then controls his will.

The Positive Correlation of Evil to Goodness

This chapter shows exactly how evil and the work of the devil (here the Witch), can be used for good by God. This is not due to an equality between good and evil because Christianity is not a dualistic religion. Evil and goodness cannot be equal. Here evil functions much more as judge and executioner, but is still subordinate to the law, God's law.

This is not a new idea. In the book of Job, Satan is already displeased with the agreement when he is not seen as prosecutor. The Witch and evil powers are subordinate to the law of love. This demonstrates that love is not just an ethical commandment, but instead love is what sustains humanity and the universe. The consequence of denying love – as in broken relationships – is no different to death and therefore no different to that which people choose for themselves. Thankfully, although He cannot blot them out, God in his faithfulness can limit the harmful consequences of sin to His creation. Were He to do this, He would be breaking the conditions by which man exists as man and God would cease to be God. The world would them simply be chaos. If the law of love has no sanctions then there would be something far worse in its place namely dualism of good and evil as equal. Evil and chaos would rule together. So in order to avoid this, evil functions as a sanction when the law of love is violated.

Rejection of the Naturalistic Fallacy

Since Christianity values the double-commandment of love as so strong, it sets itself apart from a philosophical view, which is very old and was picked up by David Hume, that an "ought" (should) cannot come out of a "to be". The fact that a tree stands in a field does not mean to say that a tree should be there. From sentences in which "to be" occurs, sentences including "should" or "shall" do not arise. This seems to be pure logic. If this theory were true, it would ultimately mean that existence or natural circumstances are independent of ethics. The analytical philosopher John Searle could show, that because of a false conclusion this doctrine is not true and that it is also possible and logical to derive "should" sentences from sentences which do not contain them.[62] Also Christianity would be incomprehensible if it was not taken for granted that issues about existence and ethics do not belong closely together as is shown in the "double commandment" of love.

The Deep Original Magic and the
Double-Imperative of Love as Law

In the beginning, love had no legal aspect. Love is the principle by which the universe exists. Love holds everything in the world together. However, in order for love to be authentic it must be spontaneous and therefore would include freedom and the possibility of this freedom being abused. Once this abuse happens, love is not destroyed, but is changed to include a command. It now contains a "thou shalt" component, which man cannot obey perfectly no matter how hard he tries. This imperfect love carries with it a sanction. Violated love, that is betrayal, demands a price, ultimately punishment by death.

C.S. Lewis included all of these Christian ideas in the Deep Magic from the Dawn of Time, and engraved on the stone table that treachery demands blood. These ideas are seen throughout history. The double-commandment of love comes from Old Testament law. The Ten Commandments were engraved on stone tablets and upheld by Moses, in the same way the Deep Magic is engraved on the stone table. The first three commandments on the first tablet represent the first half of the double-commandment, namely loving God. The following seven, the so-called second tablets are about love for one's neighbour.[63] Therefore the stone table represents that which Christianity calls the old covenant. The Deep Original Magic on the stone table and the Ten Commandments on the stone tablets fit together.

Can Love that demands Death truly be Love?

In theory this is all well and good, but can a love, which when violated demands death really be love? What kind of God claims to be love itself and then has such dreadful laws? Did He have to have such a law? Could He not have created humanity and the universe with other rules? These are the kinds of questions asked and they are the questions theologians and philosophers have asked through the ages. In this chapter we see this when Lucy asks if there is not some way of working against the Deep Magic in order to save Edmund. Aslan's answer simply indicates that this is the Emperor's will (page 151).

His answer can be compared to a medieval debate, with various resolutions that has a very definite resolution. This debate asks, does God want goodness because it is good (perseitas boni) or is goodness good, because it is what God decrees (perdeitas boni)?[64]

C.S. Lewis settles for the latter – goodness is good because God wants it to be. If God had wanted something else, then whatever else He had decided on would have been goodness. Then love, or the Deep Magic, would not have had to be only the law, but instead that which God had always wanted was good and therefore the law. God cannot simply change that which He has always wanted because God cannot contradict Himself. According to this view, God could have wished something else but whatever He had willed would also have had a structure of rules and laws, because if it were designed to be completely free of rules it would have resulted in chaos and this would no longer reflect the character or the will of God. Pure chaos, as has already been mentioned, would be evil and completely separate from anything good.

Of course there is the other answer. God wants goodness because it is good. Is goodness therefore independent from God? That cannot be the case, if goodness itself is identical with God, as in Neo-Platonic thought. If goodness is love and if love means relationship, then God is eternally love because he exists in the community of relationship that is the Trinity – Father, Son and Holy Spirit and this was so even without the creation of a world.[65] When God decides to create a world what could be more logical than God giving this world His own character – the character of love?

C.S. Lewis implies this view in this chapter. He refers to the

Deeper Magic as older than Narnia and the world itself, which must mean the Deep Magic is anchored in the Emperor and his relationship with Aslan.

However we look at the arguments the Deep Magic cannot easily be overruled. Is Edmund then lost after all? We already know that the Witch has renounced her claim on Edmund's life because of a promise made by Aslan. In the next chapter this promise will be revealed in its entirety.

The Triumph of the Witch

This chapter presents powerful parallels to the passion of Christ. At the end of the previous chapter the reader learns that Aslan does not let on his promise to the Witch. He gives the order to decamp, saying the place of the stone table will be needed for other purposes, and Peter must prepare for the battle as leader of Aslan's army. Peter states that of course Aslan will be there himself, but he says he cannot promise to be there (page 154).

By the time they have set up camp night has fallen and everyone is affected by Aslan's mood. Susan and Lucy cannot sleep and they think this is because of Aslan's melancholy mood, so they decide to get up and have a look around. They discover Aslan quietly and secretly leaving the camp. The two girls follow him and on being discovered they ask if they can go with him wherever he is going. He agrees to this, but only as long as they do as he says. If he tells them to, they have to stop and leave him to go on alone.

During their walk the children put their hands on Aslan's mane, so he can feel he is not alone. Once they are near the stone table again, he tells them they must not come any further, so the girls watch shocked and tearful as Aslan goes to the Witch and all those on her side, ogres, poisonous mushrooms and spirits, who are obviously awaiting his arrival. As he reaches the stone table, the Witch calls him a fool and gives the order for him to be bound and shaven. The evil crowd mock Aslan, saying he is no more than a big cat (page 160).

Lastly the Witch sharpens her knife, telling him he will not have saved Edmund at all and what a fool he is for offering himself in Edmund's place. When she has killed him, who will stop her from killing Edmund as well and reigning over Narnia forever? She declares that Aslan has lost his own life and not saved Edmund's and in this knowledge he is to despair and die. Finally the Witch kills Aslan as the children look away (page 163).

Subjective and Objective Atonement

The chapter we have here parallels the passion of Christ, but the Narnia stories as a whole accomplish much more. They do not just explain the biblical stories in the context of a fantasy world, but they deliver philosophical and theological interpretations as well. This chapter recreates the passion of Christ. Aslan, like Jesus, suffers a violent death and this poses the question of how such a violent death can assure salvation for humanity, or in Narnia, the children and the animals. Throughout the course of the history of ideas there have been numerous answers to this question, which we will now discuss one by one to see how the presentation of redemption or atonement fits in.

At this point we turn our attention to one particular aspect. Is what happened on the cross a subjective or objective outcome, or both? This needs further explanation. By an objective outcome, we mean something, which changes and influences the world, without people subjectively knowing about it. We can understand Jesus' death in this way. The cross is something that changed the whole world, even if no one recognised this. However, we could also say that nothing objective happened on the cross, but instead only something subjective, which had meaning for the people who saw Jesus hanging on the cross or the people who have had the crucifixion explained to them. They could see for example that God Himself suffers with us and does not leave us alone. This is how people develop passion and thankfulness and love for God. This would be a purely subjective event. Naturally both are possible.

We see that Lewis thought of this right at the beginning of this chapter (page 153). "Of course everyone was dying to ask him how he had arranged matters with the Witch; but his face was so stern and everyone's ears were still ringing with the sound of his roar and so nobody dared." This question alone shows which possibility Lewis chose. Even though the gospels are full of indications and references to Christ's suffering, the idea that His suffering is necessary is not found anywhere. Therefore Lewis is saying that what happens has a completely objective meaning because the children and animals do not recognise it. This means Lewis thinks that the act of salvation, atonement or reconciliation can also change the world in a completely objective way, i.e. even when no one recognises it. (We will not yet go into exactly how this happens exactly, but instead we will stay with the question of whether Jesus' violent death was subjective or objective.)

A subjective effect in people's hearts seems to be imperative. Otherwise what would be the point of Christ dying on the cross if people do not hear about it and subjectively come to faith? In modern times many theologians have emphasised that the cross of Jesus is an exclusively subjective matter. The reformed theologian Robert Dale was for objectivity. He said if we imagine a man who goes into his brother's burning house in order to save his brother's child and he manages to save the child, but the man himself dies in the flames. His brother will no doubt think of this as proof of brotherly love. Let us imagine a different scenario: The man goes into his brother's burning house, knowing there is no one there needing help and he dies. Would his brother also see this as proof of brotherly love? Hardly, instead he would probably view this as proof of insanity. This would show that this kind of sacrifice could only truly be understood as subjective if it is truly objective.[66]

Christians join in the fight

Jesus' act of atonement and reconciliation on the cross does not by any means make Christians passive. Rather it qualifies them to act in a liberated manner but dependent on doing good and fighting against evil. C.S. Lewis expresses this aspect when Aslan is preparing Peter for the up-coming battle with the Witch, which Peter will possibly have to manage alone (page 154). "'You can either fight the Witch and her crew in the wood or assault her castle', said Aslan to Peter." At this point those paying attention to detail will ask how it is possible for the children to fight the Witch? Did Mr Beaver not say that Edmund's rescue and liberating Narnia was Aslan's business, meaning that even a person with the best intentions would not be able to accomplish this whatever he did? How does that fit together?

There is a difference between acting independently and acting under another's authority. If man tries to do good out of his own strength, then he will not succeed and what he is doing, even with the best intentions, is doomed to fail and it will unintentionally serve evil. We have already seen what Luther wrote about this.[67] However, there is a change in this after Christ's act of atonement and reconciliation. If a person trusts in Christ, then He Himself is also present. His presence – man and God working together – can have different results. In certain circumstances it can mean compassion, but it can also lead to a fierce and active resistance of evil. The latter is what C.S. Lewis was thinking of. After Aslan has been sacrificed, Peter is enabled to fight against the Witch.

Gethsemane?

Peter asks Aslan if he has to fight the Witch alone and whether or not Aslan will be there. Aslan's answer is that he cannot promise this (page 154). This seems to be a significant variation on the biblical story. Does Jesus not announce his death? At this point does he not know that he will be resurrected? Of course Jesus knows he will be resurrected, but even he was not free from challenge.

In Gethsemane (Mark 14:32–52) Jesus is lonely and afraid. He says he would rather this cup – namely the crucifixion – be taken from him, but ends his prayer by saying, not his will, but the Father's will should be done. But there is an interesting difference between the passion of Christ and the story of Aslan's death. Jesus asks the disciples to keep watch with him and not to leave him alone, but they fail because they keep falling asleep, even though Jesus wakes them. This is different in Aslan's passion. Aslan does not ask Susan and Lucy to be with him in his loneliness, but they cannot sleep and so go out, find him alone and ask if they can go with him (page 156). So in contrast to the disciples, they do not fall asleep, but rather cannot sleep.

Another parallel exists in the fact that Susan and Lucy ask Aslan if they can go with him wherever he is going (page 157). This reminds us of Peter, who does not want to leave Jesus alone in exactly the same way and says he will never leave Jesus, no matter what happens, Mark 14:29–31. Here there is another interesting difference. Susan and Lucy ask Aslan if they can go with him, but Peter promises Jesus wholeheartedly, without being asked. Accordingly, the answer is different in each case. Whilst Jesus must put the self-deluded Peter in his place, by saying that no one else can do what He must do, Aslan answers differently. First he allows the children to accompany him, but they have to promise that they will leave him alone when he tells them to. Both Susan and Lucy comply with this and later obey Aslan. Once again this shows that C.S. Lewis portrays the children's role in a more positive light, than the disciples in the gospels. Jesus must ask the disciples not to leave Him alone, but the two girls take the initiative with Aslan. Obviously Aslan, like Jesus, needs to feel he is not alone because he asks the girls to lay their hands on his mane so he can feel they are with him (page 158).

This is not coincidence, but has theological significance because death is imminent. If to exist means to be in relationship, if to live means there is always dependency on another person, then death is to be completely alone.[68] Here the wish for intimacy simply expresses the wish to stay in relationship, to stay alive. And there ends our story of Gethsemane.

Is the Death of Christ what God wanted?

At this point the reader is forced to ask an important question. If Aslan does not want to die, does it really have to happen? Does the Deep Magic, which – we remember – corresponds to the double commandment of love, really have to be satisfied? And if in Gethsemane Jesus did not want to die, but only acquiesced to the Father's will, what kind of God is He who truly wants His Son to die? Does this call love into question once again? We can answer this question with an argument that we have referred to already.

According to the analytical philosopher Harry G. Frankfurt, "to want" can have two meanings. It can mean "to wish for something from the heart", which Frankfurt calls first want or it can mean "to take a higher purpose into consideration". Frankfurt calls this second order volition.[69] It is clear that neither Aslan's nor Jesus' first want is to die. That is presented just as clearly in the Narnia story as in the story of Gethsemane. In both cases they have a second order volition, the want for a higher purpose. Aslan wants to comply with the Deep Magic and Jesus with His Father's will. Therefore, the story of Gethsemane should never be misunderstood as if it were God's will, or first want, that Jesus should die on the cross. This would indeed be dreadful and shocking. The Father's will is much more of a second order volition, as is Jesus'. Both are in agreement and it is in this that their unity shows. God consists of a living relationship between Father, Son and Holy Spirit and through the cross this relationship is not disrupted.

However, if the Father's will is also a second order volition, then what is their first want? What do they really want in their hearts? Is it just the fulfilment of the law? The answer is partly yes because the law is the law of love. The answer is also partly no because it is not just about the law being fulfilled. That would not work at all, because then God would be under the law. It has much more to do with Father and Son having the same longing to see man freed from sin. And this means that man's broken relationship with God should be healed so that man is able to love. Obviously and interestingly enough, only Jesus' death can accomplish this. How this happens or can happen is another question that we must save for another time. Now it only remains to say that this happens the same way in the Narnia story. Aslan's first want is not to comply to the Deep Magic, this is his second order volition. His first want is to save Edmund and Narnia.

Scorn, Mockery and the Reviling of the Cross

Nietzsche strongly attacked and criticised Christianity. He claimed Christianity turns the best into the worst and the worst into the best. He said it is hostile because it teaches that the last shall be first, that strength means weakness and weakness actually means strength.[70] Actually this means that Christianity turns the values that can be seen in the world upside down and this is precisely what takes place on the cross in the passion story.

Paul made this point in 1 Corinthians 1:18 when he said he preaches the cross, which is a stumbling block to Jews and foolishness to the Gentiles. In the passion story this turning upside down of the values of the world is expressed through many different paradoxical pictures. Jesus rides into Jerusalem supposedly as a king, but he is not on a beautiful charger, instead he arrives on a donkey (Mark 11:1–11). Jesus is scoffed at and mocked by the soldiers. "He thinks he's king? Then he should have a crown!" So as a sign of this ridicule He wears the crown of thorns, He is whipped and the soldiers make bets for His clothes (Mark 15:16–20.24). The soldiers also shout abuse at Jesus. "If he is really God's son then he should help himself and get down from the cross." (Mark 15:32).

C.S. Lewis brings all of this into Aslan's passion story. He is a lion, apparently the King of the animals. They shear his mane, they muzzle him, spit on him and mock him. "Why he's only a great cat after all! Would you like a saucer of milk, Pussums?"

The Foolishness of the Cross: My God, my God, why have you forsaken me?

Mark's account of the passion story, at several different points expresses, the climax and foolishness of the cross much more radically. Jesus' last words are: 'My God, my God, why have you forsaken me?' (Mark 15:34). In our story this is also said, but it is the Witch not Aslan speaking.

How do we understand Jesus' words on the cross? Does it really mean that God the Father turned His back on the Son? Or does it mean something else? If God the Father had left the Son then this would mean the relationship between Father and Son had been broken. We have said that this relationship – God's divinity – is not externally visible. If these words from the cross were to be taken literally, then that would mean sin had triumphed because God's existence would have been affected. There have always been theologians who have refused to accept this viewpoint.

The Greek tradition says that God himself cannot suffer because God is unchanging. He would help himself. Does the church not teach that in Christ there are two "natures" – one divine and one human? This seems to provide a way out of this dispute. Only this human nature suffers on the cross. And the exegete, biblical theorists, could indirectly support this view. The words 'My God, my God, why have you forsaken me?' are a quotation. Jesus quotes a prayer as His last words on the cross, or more specifically, the beginning of Psalm 22. The end of the Psalm is once again comforting and full of hope and there is no sense of being left by God. Therefore, one can say, when Jesus quoted these words, He already had a sense of the end of the psalm and was already thinking of His resurrection.[71]

However we will refuse to accept this solution because it expresses how even Christians try to explain away the unreasonable demand of the cross; this incomprehensible turning upside down of all the world's values, which appears to be foolishness and folly from the perspective of normal reasoning. We cannot do this because if the Father did not leave Jesus then there was no break in the relationship. However, if death means to be without relationship, then this would mean Jesus did not suffer death on the cross. And if He did not die, then the cross is not redemption for us because it would have nothing to do with our death, as God would not have suffered with us. Therefore, there is only one solution left. Jesus really did experience what it is to be completely cut off from relationship with His Father and His words are to be taken literally.

C.S. Lewis decides on this solution in the Narnia story, but he uses a trick. He writes the story so that the Witch speaks and not Aslan. With this, he allows the sinful world to have its say about the supposed act of redemption. The Witch says unmistakably that she sees Aslan as an idiotic fool for taking Edmund's place. Aslan will die and the Witch will reign. She can simply kill Edmund and reign in Narnia forever (page 163). 'You have lost your own life and you have not saved his. In that knowledge, despair and die.' After this she kills Aslan. This expresses the world's usual opinion, that Aslan's death seems pointless, just as Jesus' death seems pointless. Obviously both deaths would be, if the stories ended there, but they do not.

Evil's Relative Independence

We have already established that evil cannot be completely independent of God and goodness because this would constitute a dualistic world-view, in which good and evil were equally powerful. If this were the case, God would not be God. We also established that evil cannot be completely dependent on God because that would mean that God was ultimately evil and therefore not good. However, we can see that there is a solution to this problem. Evil can be partly, but not completely dependent on goodnes. This is shown by the fact that God allows evil and makes use of it to fulfil the violated law of love with the punishment that follows. Obviously – and this is important – relative dependence must mean there is always relative independence and the latter is shown in the Witch's last words before she kills Aslan. The Witch used the law of love to force Aslan either to hand Edmund over or give up his own life. But in her role as the Emperor's executioner this does not mean she will abide by the law of love, and indeed she does not. After she has killed Aslan, her plan is to kill Edmund and take Narnia forever. This shows her relative independence from goodness. Evil is not reliable. C.S. Lewis describes evil's relative independence from goodness and it's fly-by-night character by drawing another parallel at the end of the last chapter. The Witch wanted confirmation that Aslan would keep his promise, but from Aslan she only gets a roar in answer (page 152) and his sacrifice in this chapter. It is different with the Witch's promise. She intends to break her promise of letting Edmund go free.

Deeper Magic from the Dawn of Time

The reader now expects the story of Jesus' death and suffering to be told and is not disappointed. After Aslan's execution, the Witch and her followers make a hasty retreat to prepare for battle against Aslan's people. When it is safe, the two girls approach the stone table where they stay awake and tearful for the whole night. As morning comes they notice small mice crawling on Aslan's body busying themselves nibbling through the cords that bind him.

Morning draws nearer, they move away from the stone table and suddenly hear a deafening noise. Startled they assume the Witch has done yet worse things to Aslan. However when they turn around the stone table is in two pieces with a crack down the middle and Aslan is not there (page 169). The girls suspect that either the enemy has taken his body or it is more magic. A confirming voice from behind them says it is more magic and when they turn around they see Aslan with a new mane (page 170). The two girls are frightened, thinking Aslan is a ghost. He tells them he is real and explains the deeper magic (page 171).

The first thing Aslan does is to play catch with the children and finally there are allowed to ride on him (page 171). Aslan takes them to the Witch's house, which she has left to go and fight Peter and the rest of Aslan's followers. In one leap Aslan jumps over the castle wall with the girls still on his back (page 174).

Care for the Dead

In this chapter a well-known biblical motif appears, namely care for Jesus body. In the gospels (Mark 15:43; Matthew 27:57; Luke 23:51; John 19:38) a rich man called Joseph of Arimathea, who is described as a disciple, comes to Pilate and asks if he may take Jesus' body and put it in his grave. It is important to note that not only the poor and despised, but also well-to-do people followed Jesus and supported his mission.

C.S. Lewis turns this caring motif upside down. It is not the strong or rich who care for Aslan, but instead the small mice that nibble through his bonds, seemingly the smallest and weakest amongst the animals (page 167). In the Narnia books that follow this story is recounted and the mice are rewarded for their act of love. They receive recognition, greatness, intelligence and, in the character Reepicheep, produce one of the most famous heroes in all the of the Narnia stories.

The Truth of the Resurrection

Jesus' bodily resurrection and him not being recognised or mistaken for a ghost is a well-known motif in the gospels. In Luke 24:36–45, the disciples think Jesus is a ghost and are frightened. Jesus shows them he is not a ghost, but flesh and blood, by showing them his wounds and eating some fish. Finally he explains to them what has happened must happen according to the Old Testament prophecies. This is similar in C.S. Lewis' story in that the children think the resurrected Aslan is a ghost, but he convinces them otherwise (page 170). In order to understand the meaning of this motif plainly, it would be sensible to firstly understand differences between Jesus' resurrection and ghosts.

1. Ghosts belong in stories where they are deemed to be real, they do not belong to our reality because they are ephemeral and only have the opportunity to appear at certain times in certain places. However, the resurrected Christ belongs to our reality, but the gospels go on to say more. After all, raising people from the dead is not something in our field of experience. But the resurrected Christ does not only belong to our reality, but as the eternal God the Son He played a role in creation and is the world's purpose. He is alpha and omega, beginning and end of the world. Therefore He defines what reality actually is. We have problems accepting this and end up understanding the resur-

rection as less real than our own reality. This is apparent in the resurrection as it is much more real than our field of experience because according to Christian understanding the reality of the resurrection reveals to us the future and the end of the world. Because we have not yet experienced our future it is just as difficult for us to understand this "final future", as it is for us to grasp the reality of the resurrection. However, this does not mean it is less real than our field of experience, but rather from this we can conclude that based on our experience we have to admit we cannot exactly say what reality truly is. Not that we can clarify the reality of the resurrection out of our reality, but the other way around.

2. The second difference between the risen Christ and ghosts is that ghosts have a raw deal. They are dead, yet not dead, and at the same time are not allowed to die because they have done something bad. They crave deliverance. Contrary to this, the resurrected Christ does not need deliverance, but instead, Jesus as risen saviour, delivers us because it is us who need it. If the risen Jesus were a ghost, he would not have had anything to do with people. Also, his act of redemption on the cross and his resurrection would not have helped us; it would not serve as salvation. In light of this Christian tradition has always rejected a movement by the name of Docetism.[72] Docetism assumed that it was not Jesus as God and man that was crucified, but tries to explain away this unsavoury fact. Say we said somebody else had been crucified, just a fake body, not really Jesus' body. Then it would have only seemed as if he had been crucified and raised again. That is where this movement gets its name, "dokeo" is Greek for "to seem/appear". If this were the case then there would never have been an event of salvation because we are physical beings. The gospels make this clear not only through stories about the physicality of the resurrection but by highlighting the wounds of the crucifixion by which the risen Jesus is identified. He has marks in his hands, feet and side, which he allows Thomas to touch (John 20:24–31). This aspect of identity remains unresolved in C.S. Lewis' story. Aslan asks a rhetor-

ical question, whether he looks like a ghost, to which the girls answer no, it is really him (page 170). How they know this is not explained, because the identity motif (the remaining marks after the resurrection), is also not discussed because Aslan's mane (shorn off before his death), appears to have grown back (page 170).

3. The third difference between the resurrected Christ and ghosts exists in the fact that ghosts are not only being punished and in a bad way themselves, but they also frighten others and want to cause them to be afraid, whereas the risen Jesus or Aslan appear in order to comfort and bring joy. The disciples' initial fear at seeing Jesus vanishes and is replaced by joy. It is a time for celebration and joyousness. C.S. Lewis shows this by Aslan delighting with the children. He plays a game of catch with them, messing around. Initially this is more important than standing by Peter in battle (page 171). This exuberance means that people can fully depend on the reality of the resurrection and the hope it shows. The risen one not only celebrates, but he comes to comfort people, free them and to give them a sustainable foundation. Jesus himself is this sustainable foundation and C.S. Lewis shows this by the children riding on Aslan's back (page 172). He carries the children just as Jesus carries people and this applies to all in justice and everything terrible that man endures. C.S. Lewis reflects this in that Aslan does not just carry this children, but also that the ride takes them to the Witch's house (page 173).

The Gospel and the Deeper Magic

The word "gospel" is not just a description of particular types of texts in the New Testament. "Gospel", "*euangelion*", literally means "good news". Martin Luther saw clearly that the gospel summarises what God does for man, whereas the law summarises what he wants man to do.[73] Therefore, the gospel and the law are opposites, but they do not contradict each other, as in they do not eliminate each other, but instead relate to each other in a positive way. The law and the gospel are the two fundamental aspects of God's word. C.S. Lewis presents this in the Narnia stories as well, where the "law" is "the deep magic from the dawn of time" and the gospel is "yet deeper magic from the dawn of time". We have to discuss the deep magic in order to understand the deeper magic.

We have already said that from a Christian point of view, the law – what God wants us to do – is summarised in the double-commandment of love. As already noted, this has two aspects: one formal and the other contextual. The contextual aspect consists of loving God and loving our neighbour. The formal aspect consists of how this love appears: as a commandment or law, "thou shalt/you should". We have already indicated that under the conditions of sin, this law cannot be fulfilled, because it commands something, namely love, which cannot be wilfully pursued, but can only be spontaneously fulfilled. Through this the law is then fulfilled and gives evil the power to punish, like with the Witch in the Narnia stories. Aslan is killed because of the deep magic, just as it is ultimately the law that causes Jesus to be crucified.[74] Jesus' act of atonement, meaning his death and resurrection, brings forth the gospel, which is partly opposed to the law. Effectively the law loses its validity. As it says in the Bible, Christ is the fulfilment as well as the end of the law (Romans 7:1, 8:2). This part of the law's power, which led to death, being broken, is expressed through the curtain in the temple ripping in two with the clap of thunder at the moment of Jesus' death (Mark 15:38). The temple represents the so-called old covenant, which is made up of the law. C.S. Lewis takes up this motif not only by the fact that Aslan not only visually dies on the old covenant, because the deep magic from the dawn of time is engraved on the stone table, but also by the stone table breaking in two with a loud clap of thunder (page 169). However this is only one side of the coin.

The law and the gospel are not and cannot be opposed to one another. It is easy to see why. The law is God given. If Jesus, who is the Son of God, were only the end of the law, then this would be a contradiction in God and the Trinity. God would stand against God, going against God existing as uncontradictory love. Moreover, if Christ were only the end of the law, man and creation would be handed over to chaos. And as this has been recognised as a sign of evil, this would mean that evil triumphed by the cross. So in the world of Narnia, the Witch would have won. But the story of the curtain ripping in the temple illustrates something very important.

The curtain to the holy of holies tears, meaning the holy of holies is open and available to all. In the cross God allows a free pathway to himself. How? This shows that the law and the gospel belong together. Both are love, love for God and love for our neighbour. Only the form is different. The "thou shalt" ceases to apply because of what Jesus does. It is replaced by the "you will be", meaning "you will love". God says this to people on the cross and the encouragement is God's promise, that people should act exactly the way he did to Jesus death, namely in revival. Revival will happen in the future, but also in the present and is shown through man being empowered, enabled and inspired by the presence of God the Holy Spirit, to love spontaneously. This is possible because of the cross.

In the Narnia story C.S. Lewis presents this by Aslan explaining the deeper magic (the gospel), to the children. "It means that though the Witch knew the Deep Magic, there is a magic deeper still which she did not know. Her knowledge goes back only to the dawn of time. But if she could have looked a little further back, into the stillness and the darkness before time dawned, she would have read there a different incantation. She would have known that when a willing victim who had committed no treachery was killed in a traitor's stead, the Table would crack and Death itself would start working backwards." (Page 171). Aslan's precise words are extremely significant in revealing Lewis' understanding of redemption. We will analyse this passage step by step.

The Witch only knows the law, not the gospel. That also

means she does not fully know the law, but only the "thou shalt". She does not really understand anything about the law of love. This is no wonder because in the form "thou shalt" she has power, when the commandment does not follow. However, Lewis' explanation of why the Witch does not understand this aspect and therefore does not understand the gospel is interesting. The Witch, like the children and the animals, is part of God's creation. She belongs to the world and can therefore only see as far back as the beginning of the world and no further. But what is before and outside of the world and time? Only God himself. God is love, which means as Father, Son and Holy Spirit they are an eternal relationship of love. Only God himself can know this and Aslan is described as son of the Emperor therefore he is God in Narnia. He knows about the love because he belongs to it himself and this makes Aslan's sacrifice comprehendible. It is a devotion to love because devotion means to be available to others in soul and body as a whole person, and committed to their welfare.[75]

Obviously this is not possible for humans for two reasons. For one thing we do not really know the appropriate means for other people's welfare. What is good for my neighbour? Is it his or her intentions, his or her own will? Or is it what I suppose to be good for him or her. In every-day life both things often differ. We cannot know this but God the Son, who is our creator, knows what is truly good for His creation.[76] The other reason why no human can be a sacrifice for any another is because one can only really devote what is one's own. We can only sacrifice for someone in love, something at our disposal; our possessions or our time. We cannot, or rather are not permitted to sacrifice ourselves as persons. Because as humans we are not independent individuals, who exist in isolation, but we are persons in relationship and all relationships are modelled on the relationship to God. Therefore man does not belong to himself but to God. If man disregards this and wants to give himself completely to another person, then he only brings forth evil and harm and thus man does not love, but only breaches the rule of love.[77]

History is full of examples of people who lose themselves in other people and nothing good comes of it. This is different with Christ. Because He Himself is God, He belongs to Himself and rules over himself. Therefore only Christ can bring this sacrifice of love and it is the same with Aslan, the Son of the Emperor.[78] Obviously we have gone beyond C.S. Lewis explanation with this because in the quotation Aslan says "when a willing victim who had committed no treachery was killed in a traitor's stead, the Table would crack and Death itself would start working backwards." (Page 171). It seems as if someone else could have been this sacrifice as long as he was innocent, or without sin. Divinity does not seem to be a condition for C.S. Lewis that is directly relevant here. Indeed our explanation does not contradict C.S. Lewis' because we can ask under what conditions is sinlessness achievable and as we have seen, under the conditions of the fall, sinlessness or perfection is no longer an option for humans. This shows that our explanation does not go beyond C.S. Lewis but rather serves to amplify it.

Some may question why this sacrifice of love should cause death to work backwards? The answer is in the end not complicated. We have already established that love is more than an ethical principle. Love is not just about actions. Love is also intrinsic to existence and being itself. Where God is love, existence and essence is love, and love is existence and essence, at least where Christians are concerned. Christ in His life on earth consistently adhered to the sacrifice of love. Man's contradiction of this leads Him to the cross, death and being cut off from relationship. But love cannot be killed in this way and it is precisely then that love remains faithful by transforming death and this absence of relationship.[79] It is no longer a place without God because God is already a part of death, whereby death ceases to be beyond relationship. God Himself is violated through the Son's death because Father and Son suffer with Him. However, because love is not violated, Jesus' resurrection is the logical result and this happens for our benefit. Because it means that death for us no longer means to be completely cut off from relationship. In death God the Son will also carry us, just as Aslan carries the children on his back, even when they are going to the Witch's house which is a symbol for death. But that is the topic of the next chapter.

What Happened to the Statues

In this chapter, Aslan and the two girls hurry to the Witch's house, whilst she and her followers are fighting Peter. In and around the whole house there are statues of animals and the other creatures she has turned to stone. Lucy also finds Mr Tumnus, who disobeyed his orders by not handing her over to the Witch. Aslan breathes life back into all of them, so they can go together and help Peter and the others fight against the Witch. They arrive just as Peter and the Witch are head to head in a sword fight. Aslan leaps onto her, she dies and her followers give up the fight.

The Descent into Hell

Christ's act of redemption on the cross is an historical event that happened at a particular place and time and this appears to create a problem. Can this also bring salvation to those who lived prior to Jesus' time? One positive answer to this question is Christ's descent into hell. The following idea answers the question of what the dead Jesus did between Good Friday and Easter, the cross and the resurrection. He descended into hell to redeem all those who died before Him, right back to Adam and Eve. This means that on Easter Day hell was empty of people. This theme can be found on numerous church altars and in many illustrations of the resurrection.[80] One often finds a sort of grotto under the cross where Adam's bones are supposed to be, or Christ is pictured bringing Adam out of hell. In the Church of the Rock in Jerusalem is a stone with a hole in it and legend states that Jesus' blood dripped through this hole on to Adam's bones and saved him. Therefore we can say the price that Jesus paid works retrospectively as well and this is hope for those who did not live in His time.

Of course this is also possible because people are not isolated individuals, but are connected with each other belonging and being important for others. Just as this idea makes sin all encompassing it also makes it possible for salvation to be universal. This is expressed in a more abstract way by Paul in Romans 5:19, with the Adam-Christ typology: "For just as through the disobedience of the one man many were made sinners, so also through the obedience of the one man many will be made righteous." Just as one brings death, another brings life.

C.S. Lewis also picks up this theme, but with one difference. Only after he has come back to life does Aslan go to the Witch's house and save all the stone statues, the symbols of death and sin. This liberation takes place as Aslan breathes on the stone figures and they come back to life (page 175). This theme is significant because it shows that C.S. Lewis sees redemption as new life. This can be explained by the second creation story in Genesis 2:7, "the Lord God formed the man from the dust of the ground and breathed into his nostrils the breath of life and the man became a living being." In the Old Testament life did not belong to men and animals but was breathed into them by God and when they died this breath, or living energy goes back to God. This is exactly what the Hebrew word for "soul" means. This differentiates the Hebrew and Greek understandings of the soul. In Greek the soul is a person's core identity, what makes them unique, but in Hebrew the soul is not individual, but a physical manifestation of this living energy. C.S. Lewis alludes to this biblical idea when Aslan revives the creatures. On the one hand this reflects Aslan's divinity, because he gives life that only God can give, and on the other hand redemption is portrayed as an analogy of creation. Just as God called the world into being in the creation without prerequisites, He also liberates humanity in the same way, without any conditions, but purely by His Grace.

Man's Co-operation and the Ability to overcome Evil

Christ's resurrection and the way it works retrospectively are not exhaustively dealt with here. The meaning of salvation is relevant for believers at all times. Believers are enabled by their actions and by love and therefore empowering them to oppose evil – something they cannot do in their own strength. C.S. Lewis shows this by Peter and Edmund and the animals being able to stand against the Witch and her army. They can take up the fight against evil, without giving in to it. Obviously it is possible for man to stand against evil, but he cannot ultimately overcome or defeat evil. Involvement in God's act of salvation is under an eschatological proviso, which means that the final overcoming of evil is something in God's future plan. Through Christ's act of redemption man is enabled to love and do good, but the whole of humanity is not perfect. This means it is not possible for humanity to become perfect without God's help, the opposite to the teachings of the Enlightenment. C.S. Lewis shows this by allowing the Witch to overwhelm the children and creatures of Narnia in battle (page 184). Peter and Edmund can resist the Witch, but the final victory belongs to Aslan and can only be won by him.

The Hunting of the White Stag

This is the last chapter of *The Lion, the Witch and the Wardrobe*. First of all the consequences of the battle are explained. In Aslan's absence it was the former traitor Edmund not Peter who played the main role in that he was insightful enough to break the Witch's wand with his sword. Edmund is badly hurt and Lucy's cordial heals him and the other wounded. Aslan frees those the Witch turned into stone during the battle. On the battlefield Aslan finally makes Edmund a knight and takes the whole company to the castle of Cair Paravel where Peter, Edmund, Susan and Lucy become Kings and Queens amongst great celebrations during which Aslan disappears unnoticed. The children grow into men and women as Kings and Queens and rule peacefully over Narnia for many years. One day they hear about a white stag that grants wishes and set off to hunt the stag and they return to the wardrobe. As they go back through the wardrobe they become children again and it is the same day and time as when their adventure first began. The children tell the professor about their adventure and he believes them.

The Effect of Healing: Justification and Sanctification

The consequences of Jesus' act of reconciliation naturally are that it makes the sinner's justification possible through grace alone, which means they are accepted without having to prove anything. The Holy Spirit can transform a person into a new person by changing their feelings because if a sinner's feelings and emotions are transformed, so is their core being. A person then becomes capable of new actions and develops a passion and love for God's purposes.[81] But it is not only feelings, desires and actions that are transformed, but also the mind, which is effected by sin, so the whole person is transformed. Lewis in his writing also describes this healing.

One can ask whether all of these transformations of the sinner are possible in a purely objective way, without there being simultaneously a subjective understanding. We referred to the cross as a purely objective act of atonement, after a world-altering objective act of salvation taking place, but people do not necessarily need to know about or experience this. On the other hand we also referred to an understanding that occurs only in people's hearts – not objectively in the world – as a purely subjective understanding of salvation. We said this was ultimately paradoxical. A subjective effect in people's hearts can only come about when something objective happens simultaneously. What about the other way round?

Interestingly C.S. Lewis seems to infer that the effects of the acquired healing – the effective transformation of a person in justification and sanctification through a purely objective understanding of atonement – can be achieved without the person appreciating it subjectively or knowing that it happens. Susan and Lucy have the following conversation (page 188): "'Does he (Edmund) know what Aslan did for him? Does he know what the arrangement with the Witch really was?' 'Hush! No, of course not,' said Susan. 'Oughtn't he to be told?' said Lucy. 'Oh, surely not,' said Susan. 'It would be too awful for him.'" Clearly Edmund hears nothing of what Aslan did for him and in this Narnia story no one says that he will ever be told. All the same, the effects of justification and sanctification appear dramatically in Edmund's behaviour. How is this possible? This remains unanswered and unexplained. It appears that Edmund transforms, without us knowing why. One cannot simply attribute it to the work of the Holy Spirit because unfortunately He plays a very understated role in this story. A purely objective comprehension of the atonement does not suffice and it cannot show how this affects people inwardly and in their actions because our actions come from our intentions and these are an inner concern. Therefore, we can conclude that both an objective and subjective comprehension of salvation are always necessary. Perhaps C.S. Lewis saw this as well, but did not express it in the story. This story is written so that adults and children can understand Christ's act of salvation. If C.S. Lewis were not convinced of salvation being objective, this would not have been necessary.

Now we come to the effects that justification and sanctification have on Edmund himself. Not only does he do what is right and fights on the right side, but he does it in an especially insightful way. He knocks the Witch's wand out of her hand and saves Narnia because all the others went for the Witch herself, not her wand, and were subsequently turned into stone (page 186). More than one theme is dealt with here. Edmund is the most insightful of them all; his foolishness and rashness have completely vanished. Perhaps this is a result not only of what Aslan did, but also the fact that Edmund is the only one who has experienced firsthand how dangerous the Witch is.

Another theme expressed here is that Edmund not only experiences healing through Aslan, but he is also capable of right behaviour which leads to him saving the others. He knocks the Witch's wand out of her hand and prevents any more animals from being turned into stone. The sinner becomes the saviour.

The third motif, handled at this point is that the effects of justification and sanctification do not mean that all suffering vanishes. Because to do good in the world, will bring resistance from the world and does inevitably also mean suffering. This is the meaning of suffering for Christ. It does not mean man should go in search of evil, but when it comes to resisting evil or sin in the knowledge of salvation and a sinner forgiven, suffering is possible. Edmund being badly wounded after his act of bravery portrays this in the story. (Page 187).

This leads directly on to the fourth theme: even justified and sanctified people do not live purely for themselves but stay with Jesus and other people who are in Christ. This expresses again the Christian understanding of humanity as interconnected. C.S. Lewis works out this theme by showing when Edmund is injured he is reliant on Lucy and her life-giving cordial to save him. This makes clear how the effects of justification and sanctification differ from person to person and are manifested in people's unique gifts and charismas. It is significant that Edmund is described very differently to Peter. Peter has become a brave and glorious fighter because of his role as leader of the army (page 192) and these are also virtues which are useful in God's Kingdom. The following shows how what Aslan did effected Edmund, the exemplary sinner, who betrayed his brother and sisters to the Witch: "Edmund was a graver and quieter man than Peter, and great in council and judgement." (Page 192.)

In this short passage C.S. Lewis manages to express Luther's understanding of justification. Luther describes his discovery of the new understanding of "God's justice" like this: God's justice is not a justice by which he shares out what everyone will get. Instead it means the power by which He creates righteous people out of sinners. Even so as God's power and wisdom means God's ability by which God makes the sinner strong and wise.[82] This is possible because God's love is different from human love. Whilst human love develops from worthiness and requires estimable characteristics, God's love does not look to find worthiness, but create it in people.[83] According to Luther, God's love is a creative love.

Empowering Humans for their Role as Ruler

We have seen how in the very beginning of history, man was in the position of ruler over the whole creation to care for and look after it. Through sin, man forfeits this position, but through Jesus' death, man is able to reassume this role. Cooperation and working with Jesus means exactly this. Man participates in Jesus' kingship, as faith describes and what the lying snake promised is fulfilled in this; man becomes like God and can work with him.

C.S. Lewis portrays this by Aslan crowning the children Kings and Queens of Narnia at Cair Paravel (page 189). Originally

Edmund mistakenly trusted the Witch's false promise and arrogantly wanted to be prince of Narnia. He achieves much more than this, without having to do anything. Edmund is a king of Narnia. Also this way of coming to power is different from other kings that we know of. This is by no means a monarch who could become an individual despot, a king who can do anything he wants, but here all the people together can demonstrate this kingship, just as we see Peter, Edmund, Susan and Lucy doing. This kingship and therefore man's destiny cannot be lost (page 189). "'Once a king or queen in Narnia, always a king or queen. Bear it well, Sons of Adam! Bear it well, Daughters of Eve!'" This honour and designation cannot be taken away because it does not depend on achieving particular and required characteristics, but instead God promises this whilst man is in a dependent relationship with God and cannot earn this place.[84]

The Interweaving of Sunday and Everyday Life

The salvation that Christians experience through Jesus is not limited to a particular time or place. Christianity overrules the old ideas that holiness is limited to particular times and places.[85] This does not mean that there are not special moments when we experience justification and sanctification, but they are not limited to these events and Christians have the job of applying what God has promised them to their everyday lives. This is exciting and also difficult. One Christian theme that reveals this is how Sunday and everyday life belong together. Sunday worship and the Church service represent a Christian's acceptance, forgiveness and relationship with God, but in every service the final blessing is a ritual which serves not just to finish the service, but to send Christians out into everyday life outside the church and into their dealings with other people and the world. These two – the church service on Sunday and serving God daily – belong together as a person's relationship with God and relationship to the world and are what constitute a human being.

C.S. Lewis reflects on this theme when, after the children have become adults in Narnia, they are sent back to England where amazingly they become children again in the same hour as when their adventure began. Their stay in Narnia has an effect on them. During this passage from Narnia back to England, where they do not yet know what awaits them, the children suspect there will be more important and exciting things everyday (page 194). "'And more,' said Queen Lucy, 'for it will not go out of my mind that if we pass this post and lantern either we shall find strange adventures or else some great change to our fortunes.'" The children's stay in Narnia represents the church service on Sunday, just as their return to England represents serving God in everyday life.

Divine Intervention and Unpredictability

Man cannot bring healing by himself, but only by working together with God, his Creator, Redeemer and Perfecter. Man remains reliant on God and after justification and sanctification is still dependent on God's healing work. The difference is that before justification man does not long specifically for salvation exactly in the way Jesus provides it, but imagines a general happiness, which can be focused on wrong and negative things. But now after salvation man longs for goodness and to be in the presence of Christ and for man it is not possible to be sure that this will always happen predictably. Where, when, how and by what means a person experiences the presence of Christ in their life remains a complete mystery for people. It has to be like this because if man could be perfectly sure where, when and how he will experience God's presence then it would not be God's presence, but something else. Man would have the power to summon God's presence and then in cooperation with it, do the right thing. But that is a contradiction, because it would mean that man could use God for his own purposes when it suited him and that man was ultimately dependent on his own ability and power not God's. This would be the opposite of what Christianity teaches about salvation. This would end in sin, individualism, separation and broken relationships and this is exactly what prevents love. We are reliant upon God's support and presence, but can never be sure where, when, how or under what circumstances we will experience this. However, this does lead us to doubt. We stand firm in the knowledge that in Jesus God is and will be with us. Knowledge is not security. We cannot describe in an orderly way when and how God will act. God remains beyond our reach and in His relationship to us He is mysterious. Therefore our destiny remains as insecure as our own identity. Who we truly are is mysterious to us.

C.S. Lewis takes up this theme of unpredictability and mystery in this last chapter. Firstly without anyone noticing Aslan disappears in the middle of the coronation celebrations for Peter, Edmund, Susan and Lucy (page 190). "And when the Kings and Queens noticed that he wasn't there they said nothing about it. For Mr Beaver had warned them, 'He'll be coming and going,' he had said, 'One day you'll see him and another you won't. He doesn't like being tied down [...] He'll often drop in. Only you mustn't press him. He's wild you know. Not like a tame lion.'"

This theme appears for the second time after the children are back in England and are explaining their adventure to the professor. He also refers to this unpredictability (page 196). "'No', he said, 'I don't think it will be any good trying to go back through the wardrobe door to get the coats. You won't get into Narnia again by that route. Nor would the coats be much use now if you did! Eh? What's that? Yes, of course you'll get back to Narnia again some day. Once a King in Narnia, always a King in Narnia. But don't go trying to use the same route twice. Indeed don't try to get there at all. It'll happen when you're not looking for it. And don't talk too much about it even among yourselves. And don't mention it to anyone else unless you find that they've had adventures of the same sort themselves. What's that? How will you know? Oh, you'll know all right. Odd things they say – even their looks – will let the secret out. Keep your eyes open. Bless me, what do they teach them at these schools!'"

Postscript: A Brief History of the Cross

Christianity teaches that Jesus' life, death and fate bring salvation for humans. Jesus' death is not isolated from his life, and it is not insignificant who died on the cross, yet the crucifixion, understood as an event bringing salvation, is very crucial for Christian belief. And precisely this seems to have been a huge unreasonable demand for humanity in the past and still is today. Critics often say, "if Christianity recognises Jesus' torturous death as salvation then it obviously glamorises death and violence. It challenges people not to resist or stand up to violence, condones violent repression, especially of women, by people who take advantage of this, and it cements these structures of violence. And what kind of God is that, for whom this sacrifice is necessary?"

This is how Christianity is attacked.[86] Such questions should be seriously addressed, even when they are brought up with strong polemics, because if the cross is really salvation then Christians must be able to explain this healing effect. This does not mean, however, that everyone has to become a Christian, but at least be able to make clear what it is actually about. One attempt at explaining this is C.S. Lewis' *The Lion, the Witch and the Wardrobe.* Through this commentary we have tried to look at Lewis' understanding of the cross. Now we must mention other ideas about what the cross means, because only then can we understand what *The Lion, the Witch and the Wardrobe* is really saying because this is one aspect of the teachings about Jesus act of atonement.

A whole host of problems with belief and also theological problems could basically be explained as the history of ideas developed, so that it is at least possible to say generally what the Christian standpoint is. This is, however, not the case with the cross of Christ, the doctrine of atonement. The church never fixed this doctrine dogmatically. There are many metaphors, pictures and models etc., which try and explain how the cross can be an act of salvation. Readers inclined to do so will then be able to classify C.S. Lewis' perception better and may then come to their own understanding of the cross. Perhaps not though, instead the opposite may happen, they may reject the cross as the act of salvation and not even take *The Lion, the Witch and the Wardrobe* as a good book or film. But even in this case, the reader will have won; there will be a fundamental reason why they have made this decision.

The Ancient Church's Doctrine of Redemption

In the ancient church there were naturally, as always, different ideas of how the cross could have a saving effect.[87] One model is particularly prominent: the model of battle and liberation. Salvation assumes harm has been caused and when one asks, how salvation comes about, then it is also dependent on how one views harm. In this model, the disaster is people's mortality, the fact that they will die. Death is described as one being a captive of dark powers, under demons and ultimately the devil. The churchfathers knew an answer to the question of why the devil has the ability to ensnare people. The devil has a certain right to hold people in death because people are sinful. But because God is good and merciful he frees us from the devil. Sometimes this is called God's battle, where Christ triumphs on the cross.

Gregory of Nyssa portrays this battle in an especially interesting way. God sends his son to earth and he looks like a man in every way, but he is brilliant and much more capable than others. He can walk on water and perform amazing miracles. Satan sees this and covets the man Jesus. He wants to bind him in death, so in his greed, Satan kills Jesus on the cross. Satan, however, does not know that Jesus was God as well as man and therefore perfect. Overlooking this he made a fatal mistake by killing Jesus because he was not allowed to do this. Therefore Satan did wrong and lost his right to sinners. He cannot hold

Jesus in death and must also release all people into the bargain. In a way this model explains how the cross can be an act of redemption.

How can we assess this model? Apart from the fact that it seems rather mystical to us as modern people, it presents problems. Firstly it is only partly biblical. Of course the Bible talks about humanity being in bondage under sin and the Bible also acknowledges that Satan is real, but Satan and the demons know exactly who Jesus is in the stories in the Bible. Indeed it is the demons, and not the disciples, who recognise Jesus for who he is, Mark 5:7. Knowing that Jesus is the Son of God does not necessarily mean believing or trusting, the above mean this model is impossible as it assumes the devil is ignorant.

This model also casts doubt on the established view of God because God should not only be thought of as loving, but should also just. However if he has to use deceit in order to save people, this does not correlate.

The Medieval Model of Trade

As we have outlined, theologians soon identified the weaknesses of this ancient church model. In the Middle Ages, Anselm of Canterbury presented a very different theory in his book *Why God became Man*, namely the doctrine of mercantile satisfaction.[88] The word "mercantile" is extremely important here, because it ultimately means, that this is a model of trade, of giving and taking. This is important to know because there are other doctrines of satisfaction. What does this particular model mean?

Everything is weighted differently. Humanity's main problem is not just death and mortality, but guilt. Humanity is guilty because God gave the world an order: to love oneself and one's neighbour. By keeping this order, humanity honours God, but by ignoring it God is robbed of his due honour and this is exactly what happens. God cannot disregard humanity's breach of the order, because then the order of creation would be pointless. Either God must punish humanity or create a balance himself, a "satisfaction". God cannot punish humanity because this would mean eternal death. Since God is love and since he made people in order to bless them, He would be untrue to himself by handing humanity over to an eternal death. But the second way of demanding "satisfaction" from humanity is impossible because humanity owes God honour for every moment of his life. If I were to receive a £1000 monthly allowance and was supposed to pay this £1000 to someone else every month, if I ever spent the money on something else I would get into debt, I have absolutely no way of paying it back. This is the same for us as we cannot afford a repayment. This leads us to a dilemma – a dead-end – but it is God's dilemma. God himself could afford to pay the price, but cannot do it himself because it must come from humanity. How does God get out of this dilemma? Very easily, he becomes man in Jesus Christ. Christ is God and therefore without sin, but as a human being he must also honour God. And he honours God in every moment of his life. Therefore he does not *have* to die, but dies freely thus offering God payment, which in turn serves to pay and overcome humanity's debt.

There are countless problems with this model. To begin with it does not explain how humanity benefits from this debt being paid. Later in the Middle Ages this question was answered, by the founding of the Treasury of the Church doctrine. The income that Jesus earned by his death is managed by the church and can be shared out between all people. One can see, at this point, that this would have triggered opposition from the reformers.

A further problematic point, which also affects our understanding of God: Is this not saying that God the Son offers God the Father "satisfaction"? This would mean that Father and Son want different things?[89] If so, surely this would jeopardise the Trinity? Anselm saw this problem and tried to solve it. It was not God the Son, offering God the Father "satisfaction" because Christ was God and man. Therefore, Christ the *man* offers Christ the *God* "satisfaction".[90] Obviously this does not really solve the problem, but only puts it aside because here it is not the unity of the trinity that is lost, but the unity of the person of the eternal Son. Is it saying that Christ was schizophrenic, and able to offer "satisfaction" as two people?

A more important problem is that this model assumes the relationship between God and humanity is like a business relationship. Humanity honours God and in return gets his blessing. But a business agreement is not founded on love. This would not be for God's sake, but about his blessing and God would not be concerned with humanity, but with world order. In a business relationship, the partners themselves are not really important to each other. For example if I am used to buying a product in a particular shop and I cannot find it there anymore, then I will go to a different shop, regardless of how charming the shop assistant might be.

The idea of a business relationship presents yet another problem. Here it is man, even when it is Jesus as man, bringing "satisfaction" voluntarily and this means producing an offering. The Reformers teach that justification is only by grace and only through Christ: man cannot do anything that will bring him nearer to God. He is to trust Christ and his work, which identifies the problem. This doctrine of atonement is based on Christ's act of atonement; if we explain this act as mercantile satisfaction we have a problem. Because then a voluntary offering out of man's capability, even if from Jesus as man, would be the basis of justification, that all other people would receive having done nothing. This would be a contradiction. The reformers could not accept this and suggested other meanings for how Jesus' death brought salvation.

The Reformation Doctrine of Penal Satisfaction

Among these other ideas, a modification of the old mercantile "satisfaction" model stands out. By leaving out one aspect – Jesus' voluntary death – the whole model changes. During his life, Jesus fulfilled everything that was important in active obedience to the father, but is passively obedient in his suffering and death. Death is not an offering that Jesus could or could not have brought. It happens because of a promise and in accordance with the Father's will, as a substitute for humanity's punishment. That means, it is not about a business relationship any more, but a legal relationship of rights and justice. Luther reflects this model with dramatic and frank words in his interpretation of Galatians 3:12: "The doctrine of the gospel [...] speaketh nothing of our works or of the works of the law, but of the inestimable mercy and love of God towards most wretched and miserable sinners: to wit, that our most merciful Father, seeing us to be oppressed and overwhelmed by the curse of the law, and so to be holden unto the same, that we could never be delivered from it by our own power, sent His only Son into the world, and laid upon Him the sins of all men, saying, Be Thou Peter, that denier; Paul that persecutor, blasphemer, and cruel oppressor; David, that adulterer; that sinner which hath did eat the apple in Paradise; that thief which hanged upon the cross; and, briefly, be Thou the person which hath committed the sins of all men. See, therefore, that Thou pay and satisfy for them." Here now cometh the law, and saith, I find Him a sinner, and that such a one as hath taken upon Him the sins of all men, and I see no sins else but in Him, therefore let Him die upon the cross; and so he setteth upon Him the sins of all men, and I see no sins else but in Him, therefore let Him die upon the cross; and so he setteth upon Him, and killeth Him. By this means the whole world is purged and cleansed from all sins, and so delivered from death and all evils."[91]

This model has difficulties which were widely discussed following the Reformation period. Initially from a religious community, the Sozinian's, then during the Enlightenment and in modern times this came up against familiar objections:[92] 1. Is guilt no longer non-transferable? Is it not bound to the guilty party? If that is the case, how can someone take another person's guilt upon himself and suffer for it? 2. Guilt cannot be taken away through worldly punishment. Death as punishment does not mean an injustice is gone from the world, but that more has been added. 3. When in this sense, sin is expiated and justice is done, it would not explain why, after Jesus' death, man is no longer a sinner. With Jesus' act of atonement, not only is guilt balanced out, but it must show why humanity's sin is truly overcome. 4. The model of satisfactory punishment or penal satisfaction presents the relationship between God and humanity as an open judicial relationship. God is the primary judge and man is subject to him. But a relationship with God must be more than a legal relationship? Does love play a role?

The Change in Doctrines of Atonement at the Start of Modern Times

These queries were not taken up all at once in the aftermath of the Reformation. Firstly the punishment model is modified further. The theologian and lawyer Hugo Grotius indicates that punishment has other functions apart from balancing out justice.[93] For instance it can protect the environment from evil or it can have an educational function by showing that someone did something wrong and what must therefore happen to them. Punishment as protection cannot be applied to the reconciliation between God and man, but its educational function is a possibility and this was the first change.

In the cross man sees clearly that sin leads to absolute death. Christ's innocently dying for others teaches humanity a moral lesson. Yet it does not solve the difficulties of guilt being nontransferable or further suffering of an innocent party. In the aftermath of the Reformation the idea of punishment was abandoned, but not the idea of education.

People remembered that Abaelard, a medieval theologian, had already, rather casually, introduced another meaning for the cross:[94] the Son's death on the cross is a sign of divine love, because God himself suffers with us and this sign of divine love prompts our thankfulness and love. His view was the catalyst for many subjective teachings on redemption. Abaelard's model also clarifies why humanity benefits from Christ's suffering. But it is not perfect either. Is God just a teacher and is the cross of Jesus only one of many methods of education? Then overcoming suffering and sin would be man's job. This correlates to the idea of humanity being able to be morally perfect in the Enlightenment and the idea of the so-called "natural religion", according to which the roots of all religion lie in ethics, morals and good behaviour. The Enlightenment taught that people are capable of morally good behaviour and that it is therefore possible for humanity to morally perfect itself. However, this meant that the Christian teachings of sin, according to which man is sinful, became superfluous. It is easy to see that this kind of model cannot apply to the reality of our existence. Even Kant, at the end of the Enlightenment, turned back to the concept of evil being rooted in humanity. His view was that every person could recognise what is good by his reason. But Kant also observed that man does not do what is good, at least not always, which again was the radical evil Kant spoke about.[95]

At the beginning of the twenty first century, we have become much more sceptical. People deny the idea that man can tell what is good using reason and from nature. What is good, is not visible and different people, cultures and communities come to different conclusions.

In analysing the Narnia story, we alluded to a further difficulty of purely subjective doctrines of atonement. A subjective effect is only possible when alongside an objective event. If I die in the fire saving my brother's child, he can see the focus of my love. But if I run into a fire in an empty house and die anyway, my brother would not see it as proof of my love, but proof that I am mad.[96]

The Abandonment of Possible Solutions

In the face of the above mentioned difficulties, can the cross possibly have a positive, explainable meaning as salvation? Or would it be better to avoid defining it? In the Late Middle Ages the latter was considered. After John Duns Scotus, who thought faith was a matter of will, it was thought that there could be no reasonable explanation for why the cross should bring salvation.[97] This did not mean the cross itself was denied as an act of salvation, but people tried to find rational arguments for why the cross should not be explained. Would not have one drop of God's blood sufficed to redeem humanity? Could not God have chosen a different way of effecting salvation or made it impossible for human beings to comprehend redemption? If we answer these questions in the affirmative, only one answer remains for why it happened the way it happened – because God *wanted* it that way. We cannot understand God's reason. Avoiding explanation achieves nothing because we imagine the relationship between man and God in a certain way. It would be the relationship of a tyrannical, despotic ruler and his subjects, but this on it's own would not suffice. God cannot be viewed only as having an all-powerful will. He must be seen as justice and love as well.

Possible Solutions through Combined Metaphors

Apart from what we have looked at with regard to different meanings of the cross throughout history, there are several other approaches. The reformers did not only think in terms of penal satisfaction. Luther exemplifies this well. Certainly he knew other models. In his "A Treatise on Christian Liberty" he formulates the idea of *admirabile commercium*. Christ and humanity's relationship is like that of husband and wife.[98] In a marriage everything is shared – in the same way Christ takes on humanity's guilt. Thus humanity receives salvation. Christ is always with us (humanity) so we are no longer separated and alone. This model more comprehensively elucidates the God-man-relationship as a love relationship. It still does not explain the cross as salvation, however.

If Christians do not address the choice of explaining salvation – because abstaining from an explanation is an explanation in itself – then they can be guided by the reformers and the Bible on this important point. In the Bible there are many metaphors, explanations and illustrations. However, simply repeating biblical stories would not suffice. It is rather about developing a model that incorporates many ideas and makes sense of them in a comprehensible way. This is in order to evaluate different aspects and images and to query if they belong together. Advantages and disadvantages can thus be distinguished. To a certain extent one can go back to the traditional models through which one would get a more general perception of what salvation in Jesus Christ really means. Each model can only describe certain aspects, in the same way that a windtunnel model of a car must show the shape, but cannot be driven itself. All this can be done via theories and the development of theories, which is how theologians usually approach a subject matter nowadays. Yet one can also come up with interpretations and theological explanations by way of writing stories. And this is exactly what C.S. Lewis has done in his Chronicles of Narnia.

Endnotes

1 Eustachius appears in *The Voyage of the Dawn Treader* and in the other Narnia stories except *The Horse and His Boy* and *The Magicians Nephew.*

2 Strictly speaking "the fall" is not mentioned in Genesis 2, because the word sin is not mentioned. However this has traditionally become known as "the fall". Clearly something happens here that influences everything that comes after it. The same happens when Edmund meets the White Witch. Sin is not mentioned here either, but is implied or can be interpreted.

3 BSLK 560.

4 Lewis, C.S.: The Four Loves, London 1960.

5 Pöhlmann, H.G.: Abriß der Dogmatik, Gütersloh [5]1990, 196.

6 Brümmer, V.: The Model of Love, Cambridge 1993, 39–56 and Ortega y Gasset, J.: On Love. Aspects of a Single Theme, London 1958, 50.

7 Herms, E.: Luthers Auslegung des Dritten Artikels, Tübingen 1987, 77ff.

8 Härle, W.: Dogmatik, Berlin/New York 1995, 434ff.

9 Anselm v. Canterbury, Cur Deus Homo – Warum Gott Mensch geworden, lat.–dt. ed. by F.S. Schmitt, Darmstadt 1956, 50ff.

10 Martinek, M.: Wie die Schlange zum Teufel wurde (StOR 37), 1996.

11 Mühling, M.: Gott ist Liebe, Marburg [2]2005, 11–15.

12 Menne, A.: Einführung in die formale Logik, Darmstadt 1985, 36.

12 Regarding Neopositivism see Wölfel, E.: Der Positivismus als Frage an die Theologie, in Beyschlag, K./Maron, G./Wölfel, E. (ed.), Humanitas – Christianitas, FS W. v. Loewenich, Witten 1968, 257–275.

14 Keuth, H.: Popper, RGG[4], vol. 6, Tübingen 2003, 1492f.

15 Menne, A.: Einführung in die formale Logik, Darmstadt 1985, 92.

16 Evers, D.: Naturgesetz I. RGG[4], vol. 6, Tübingen 2003, 115.

17 Wölfel, E.: Endet die Zeit? in: Stock, K. (ed.), Zeit und Schöpfung. Gütersloh 1997, 11–40.

18 Mühling, M.: Gott ist Liebe, Marburg [2]2005, 304.

19 Stegmüller, W.: Das Universalienproblem einst und jetzt, Darmstadt [3]1974.

20 Popper, K.R.: Über die Drei–Weltenlehre, in Popper, K.R., Objektive Erkenntnis, Hamburg 1972.

21 Schütt, H.–P.: Kausalität, RGG[4], Bd. 4, Tübingen 2001, 907–909.

22 ibd.

23 Runggaldier, E.: Was sind Handlungen, Stuttgart 1996, 144ff.

24 Mühling, M.: Fiducia, RGG⁴, vol. 3, Tübingen 2000, 115f.

25 Mühling, M.: Versöhnendes Handeln – Handeln in Versöhnung, Göttingen 2005, 58–60.

26 Sammons, M.C.: Der Reiseführer durch Narnia, Moers 1998, 23f.

27 Herms, E.: Luthers Auslegung des Dritten Artikels, Tübingen 1987, 77ff.

27 Pöhlmann, Abriß der Dogmatik, Gütersloh ⁵1990, 118f.

29 Schleiermacher, F.D.E.: Der christliche Glaube, ed. M. Redeker, Berlin 1960, vol. 1, 23–41.

30 Thomas Aquinas, Summa Theologiae, I, 2,3.

31 Pannenberg, W.: Systematische Theologie, vol.1, Göttingen 1988, 207–282.

32 Schwöbel, Chr.: Gesetz und Evangelium, RGG⁴, vol. 3, Tübingen 2000, 862–867.

33 This is the case in Martin Kähler, for instance, an influential theologian of the late 19ᵗʰ century. Cf. Mühling, M.: Versöhnendes Handeln – Handeln in Versöhnung, Göttingen 2005, 105ff.

34 The best survey here is still: Donner, H.: Geschichte Israels und seiner Nachbarn in Grundzügen, 2 vol., Göttingen 1984 and 1986.

35 Jenson, R.W.: The Triune God, in Jenson/Braaten, Carl E. (ed.), Christian Dogmatics, Philadelphia 1984, vol. 1, 87–97.

36 ibd.

37 Schwöbel, Chr.: Gott in Beziehung, Tübingen 2002, 25–51 and Mühling, M.: Gott ist Liebe, Marburg ²2005, 307–326.

38 Schwöbel, Chr. (ed.), Trinitarian Theology Today, Edinburgh 1995, 3.

39 Mühling, M.: Versöhnendes Handeln – Handeln in Versöhnung, Göttingen 2005, 214–216.

40 Schwöbel, Chr.: Gott in Beziehung, Tübingen 2002, 162.

41 Augustin, Tractatus in Evangelium Iohannis, 43,7f.

42 BSLK 507ff.

43 Mühling, M.: Why Does the Risen Christ Have Scars? Why God did not immediately create the Eschaton: Goodness, Truth and Beauty, in IJSTh 6 (2004), 185–193, 185f.

44 Luther, M.: WA 18, 685.

45 Fankfurt, H.G.: Willensfreiheit und der Begriff der Person, in Bieri, P. (ed.), Analytische Philosophie des Geistes, Weinheim 1981, 287–302.

56 Cf. the paragraph on fascinosum and tremendum in Otto, R., Das Heilige, München 2004.

47 Härle, W.: Dogmatik, Berlin 1995, 62.

48 Veltri, G.: Lilith, RGG⁴, vol. 5, Tübingen 2002, 373.

49 Wölfel, E.: Welt als Schöpfung, München 1981, 20–35.

50 Brümmer, V.: Was tun wir, wenn wir beten, Marburg 1985, 40–44.

51 Härle, W.: Luthers Zwei–Regimentenlehre als Lehre vom Handeln Gottes, in MJTh I, 1987, 12–32.

52 Ebertz, M.N./Mühling, M.: Charisma, RGG⁴, vol. 2, Tübingen 1999, 112–116.

53 Sölle, D.: Gott und das Leiden, in: Welker, M. (ed.), Diskussionen über Jürgen Moltmanns Buch "Der gekreuzigte Gott", München 1979.

54 Hutter, M.: Parsismus, RGG⁴, vol. 6, Tübingen 2003, 947f.

55 Oort, J.v.: Manichäismus, RGG⁴, vol. 5, Tübingen 2002, 732–741.

56 Goethe, J.W.: Faust I, Stuttgart 1986, 39.

57 Brecht, B.: Geschichten von Herrn Keuner, Frankfurt/M. 2004.

58 Mühling, M.: Versöhnendes Handeln – Handeln in Versöhnung, Göttingen 2005, 313.

59 ibd., 204.

60 Thomas Aquinas, Summa Theologiae, II 2,3.

61 Barth, K.: KD IV/2, § 65, 423ff.

62 Searle, J.: How to Derive "Ought" from "Is", in Foot, P. (ed.), Theories of Ethics, Oxford 1979, 101–114.

63 Peters, A.: Kommentar zu Luthers Katechismen, Bd. 1, Göttingen 1990, 87f.

64 Gilson, E./Böhner, P.: Die Geschichte der christlichen Philosophie, Paderborn 1937, 579f.

65 Mühling, M.: Gott ist Liebe, Marburg ²2005, 328.

66 Dale, R.W.: The Atonement. 24th edition after the 7th, London 1905, 52.

67 Cf. Luther's Heidelberg Disputation in WA 1, 355–365.

68 Jüngel, E.: Tod, Gütersloh 1979, 145.

69 Fankfurt, H.G.: Willensfreiheit und der Begriff der Person, in Bieri, P. (ed.), Analytische Philosophie des Geistes, Weinheim 1981, 287–302.

70 Nietzsche, F.: Der Antichrist, Abschn. 18, Werke VI/3, 183.

71 Schleiermacher, F.D.E.: Der christliche Glaube, ed. M. Redeker, Berlin 1960, vol. 2, 130.

72 Löhr, W.: Doketismus, RGG⁴, vol. 2, Tübingen 1999, 925–927.

73 Schwöbel, Chr.: Gesetz und Evangelium, RGG⁴, vol. 3, Tübingen 2000, 862–867.

74 Dale, R.W.: The Atonement, see above, 350f.

75 Mühling, M.: Versöhnendes Handeln – Handeln in Versöhnung, Göttingen 2005, 328f.

76 ibd., 331.

77 ibd., 331f.

78 ibd., 174f.

79 ibd., 333f.

80 Wichelhaus, M.: Auferstehung, kunstgeschichtlich, RGG[4], vol. 1, Tübingen 1998, 926f.

81 BSLK 661.

82 Luther, M.: WA 54, 186f.

83 Luther, M.: WA 1, 365.

84 Härle, W.: Dogmatik, Berlin 1995, 433f.

85 Mühling, M.: Profanität, RGG[4], vol. 6, Tübingen 2003, 1677.

86 e.g. Strobel, R.: Gekreuzigt für uns – zum Heil der Welt?, in Luibl, H.J./Scheuter, S. (ed.), Opfer, Zürich 2001, 125–130.

87 Wenz, G.: Geschichte der Versöhnungslehre in der evangelischen Theologie der Neuzeit, vol. 1, München 1984, 56–62.

88 Anselm v. Canterbury, Cur Deus Homo – Warum Gott Mensch geworden, lat.–dt. ed. F.S. Schmitt, Darmstadt 1956.

89 Brümmer, V.: The Model of Love, Cambridge 1993, 195f.

90 Anselm v. Canterbury, Cur Deus Homo – Warum Gott Mensch geworden, lat.-dt. hg. v. F.S. Schmitt, Darmstadt 1956, 146f.

91 Luther, M.: cited after Dale, R.W. The Atonement, see above, 350f.

92 Wenz, G.: Geschichte der Versöhnungslehre, vol. 1, see above, 119ff.

93 ibd., 128ff.

94 Vgl. Dale, R.W.: The Atonement, see above., 346.

95 Wenz, G.: Geschichte der Versöhnungslehre, vol. 1, see above, 223f.

96 Dale, R.W.: The Atonement, see above., 52.

97 Ritschl, A.: Die christliche Lehre von der Rechtfertigung und Versöhnung, vol. 1, Bonn ²1882, 73ff.

98 Cf. Martin Luther in his treatise "Von der Freiheit eines Christenmenschen", WA 7, 20–38.

Glossary

A

Abaelard, Peter, (1079–1142), medieval theologian, known for his theological reflections, notably his subjective understanding of atonement; his love affair with Heloise and his conflict with Bernhard of Clairvaux; he lectured in Paris

Actions, Godly and human actions are different. Ultimately people act according to their knowledge, particular rules, standards and duties, they choose goals and through various means endeavour to achieve them

Ahriman, evil god in parseism, the ancient Persian religion, which influenced → Manichaeism

Ahura Mazda, creator god in Parseism

Allegory, the representation of a subject in a story where every word is used to illustrate deeper truths. E.g.: In the Early church and in the Middle Ages the love spoken of in the Old Testament book *Song of Soloman* symbolised Christ's relationship to the church or to each individual

Anselm of Canterbury, Saint, medieval theologian, died in 1109, became Archbishop of Canterbury, known for his conflicts with English kings about the appointing of bishops, for his ontological argument for the existence of God and for his → teachings on mercantile fulfilment/ satisfaction

Apocalyptic, teachings from the book of Revelation about the end-times, a pessimistic view of how the world will end

Aristotle, (ca. 384 – ca. 322), Greek Philosopher, "the" medieval philosopher because of his ideas about logic and existence

Assurance, different from safety; assumptions which cannot be empirically proven, but on which every person has to depend to do anything

Augustine, Aurelius, (354–430), north African theologian, most important western theologian of ancient times, known above all for his "Confessions"

B

Barth, Karl, (1886–1968), Swiss reformed theologian, most influential Protestant theologian of the 20th century; main work: "Church Dogmatics"

Bernhard of Clairvaux, (1090–1159), medieval theologian, mystic and monk, he

preached on the second crusade and was an adversary of
→ Abaelard

C

Christology, the branch of theology treating the person of Christ as truly God and truly man, first established as Christian dogma in Chalzedon in 354

Christ's part in creation, concept according to which the world was made by and through the eternal "logos", God the Son

Cooperation in overcoming violence, man's ability to restrict violence in the knowledge that the ultimate conqueror is God

Cooperation in sustaining creation, man's duty and ability to take part in God's sustaining work in the knowledge that the ultimately responsibility for sustaining life is God's

Cosmic dimension of sin, that the effects of sin are not just limited to human beings and ethics, but also have an effect on the natural world

Craving concupiscence, a form of → Desire, understood as negative, because it focuses on the wrong goals

D

Dale, Robert William, (1829–1895), English reformed theologian, wrote extensively on Christ's atoning death; proponent of the → objective teachings on Atonement

Daughters of Eve, description of female humans in the Chronicles of Narnia; indicates that all humans belong together

Desire, human longing for what one does not have, satisfying this the object of desire can be understood as positive or negative; a component of human love

Docetism, heretical ancient church doctrine according to which Christ's body was not human, but only seemed so

Double command of love, command to love God and one's neighbour, which → sums up the whole law

Dualistic Religions, Religions which hold to the theory that God is equally good and equally evil, often the theory states there are two god's; was rejected by Christianity

Duns Scotus, John, (1256–1308), Scottish medieval theologian, buried in Cologne, involved in Voluntarianism

Duty ethics, reflection on human actions, concentrating on values, norms and duties

E

Emotions (Feelings/Affections), along with will and reason, affections are the third spiritual aspect of a person, often understood as the central part of a person's personality

Empiricism, philosophical belief that knowledge can be derived only from logic, mathematics and experience

Erskine of Linlathen, Thomas, (1788–1870), Scottish reformed lawyer, major landowner and theologian, innovative on the subject of the meaning of Christ's death

Eschatology, the part of theology concerned with death and final destiny

Ethics, the study of human conduct, motives and purposes

Ethics of goods, reflection on human moral behaviour, which concentrates on the goals of behaviour

F

Fallacy, naturalistic, widely discussed ethical problem: "should" does not follow "is"

Falsification, method of checking scientific theories imagining circumstances where they could be wrong

Fear of God, man's relationship to God, according to → Augustine and Bernhard of Clairvaux can be understood as a servant's fear (dread) or a chidlike fear (trust/respect)

G

General awareness of God, either an in-built or acquired awareness of God, meaning general characteristics, not a clearly defined God, are recognised

Gregory of Nyssa, (331–394), Bishop of Nyssa in Cappadocia, eastern theologian along with Gregory of Nazianzus and St. Basil, he was once of the three great Cappadocians. He made important changes to the liturgy; influential teachings on the Trinity and certain ancient church teachings according to which God conquers the devil by tricking him

Grotius, Hugo, (1583–1645), Dutch reformed theologian, lawyer and historian. Adherent of an Armenian theological standpoint that dismisses the doctrine of predestination and is therefore condemned by strict Calvinism. Tried to promote Christ's death as an educational punishment

H

Hegel, Georg Wilhelm Friedrich, (1770–1831), German philosopher of Idealism

Hume, David, (1711–1776), English philosopher of → Empiricism

I

Immanence (of God), God's existence/presence in the world

Individualism, the principle of being self-determined and self-reliant

Incarnation, the embodiment of the eternal logos or God the Son in human flesh as Jesus Christ

J

José Ortega y Gasset, (1883–1955), Spanish philosopher, influenced by German philosophy in the early 20th century, politically active, turned against → Individualism and Collectivism ("I am I and my circumstances"), expressed love as "exclusive attention"

K

Kant, Immanuel, (1724–1804), German philosopher, end of the Enlightenment and beginning of Idealism; his three critiques deal with the subjects of epistemology (theory of knowledge), ethics and aesthetics

L

Law and Gospel, important principles e.g. in Luther's theology. Law = what God wants man to do; Gospel = what God does for man; the law says "you should love",

the gospel says "you will love"

Love, the concept used to describe among others the attitudes of desire, of good-will and the reciprocal relationships of friendship (including romantic relationships), parent-child relationships, sibling relationships; theologically understood as the very being of God and hence of his creation

Lilith, female demon of Jewish folklore (Talmud), who practices sexual seduction; cited by C.S. Lewis as the White Witch's ancestral mother

Logos, the second person of the Trinity, God the Son, in whom Jesus became man

Luther, Martin, (1483–1546), German theologian, reformer, resurrected the teachings on justification, according to which man is accepted by God ("justified") not by works but by faith in the grace of God in Christ

M

Manichaeism, founded in Persia by Manes, (216–276), a dualistic religion with elements from Parseeism, Christianity and Buddism, died out in Europe and Asia by the Middle Ages → Augustine was involved with it before his conversion

N

natural theology, theology according to which all people can know God through their own reason

Neopositivism, early 20th century school of philosophy according to which only observable, logically demonstrable "statements of protocol" made sense and subjective world views should be disregarded; leading figure – Rudolf Carnap (1891–1970)

Neoplatonism, Plotinus (205–270) revived Platonism – a synthesis of elements from the philosophies of Plato and Aristotle with strong religious overtones; the most influencial later classical movement until the Middle Ages and Idealism

Nietzsche, Friedrich, (1844–1900), German philosopher, known for his contempt for Christianity, hugely influential post-modern philosopher → often connected with Nihilism

Nihilism, negative doctrine claiming there is no point, no truth and no standards

Nominalism, doctrine stating that universals or general ideas are abstractions from individual objects and, hence are merely names. Opposite to → Realism a)

O

objective atonement/redemption, an understanding of Christ's death whereby the world is changed objectively and salvation can have an effect without anyone being aware of it

Obsession, state in which a person is infatuated with or focuses "exclusive attention" on an object or another person; from → José Ortega y Gasset's interpretation of → Love

order of creation, different to the → order of salvation God's work as creator and sustainer of the world and in relation to it's existence,

order of salvation, different from the → order of creation, God's work in overcoming sin and the fulfilment of his work in creation

Organism, all human beings belonging together as a species and being in relationship with one another

Otto, Rudolf, (1869–1937), German religious theorist, thought "holiness" was the common aspect of religion, that a numinous secret simultaneously facinates and terrifies

P

Phenomenology, the science of phenomena

Plato, Greek philosopher, (428/7–348/7), extremely

influential throughout the history of ideas

R

Realism, a) doctrine that universal or general ideas have an objective existence; opposite to → Nominalism; b) the doctrine that the objects of perception exist independently of the perceiver; opposite of → Relativism

Reformation, the 16th century movement aimed at reforming western Christianity; led by Martin Luther, Huldrich Zwingli, Johannes Calvin and others

Relativism, philosophical attitude holding that moral value, knowledge or truth is not absolute, but relative to an individual or cultural framework

Revelation, Concept that means that God discloses Himself to a person in a particular situation as author and purpose of reality

S

Schleiermacher, Friedrich Daniel Ernst, (1768–1834), German Protestant theologian, built religion on the feeling of complete dependence ("Gefühl schlechthinniger Abhängigkeit")

Searle, John Rogers, born in 1932, American analytical philosopher, further developed J.L. Austin's Speech Act

Theory; he also studied the idea of the naturalistic → fallacy

Safety, different from → assurance a view, which sees recognition of faith as possible and available; rejected by the reformers

Scepticism, the view that truths cannot be reached through reason or experience

Seven Deadly Sins: Pride, Envy, Greed, Anger, Lust, Exorbitance, Idleness and Melancholy

Sölle, Dorothee, (1929–2003), German Protestant theologian; feminist mystic who had an impersonal picture of God; viewed the cross as compassion/sympathy

Socinianism, founded by Fausto Sozzini (1539–1604), anti-Trinitarian religious movement

Sons of Adam, description of male humans in the Chronicles of Narnia; indicates that all humans belong together

special revelation, different from → general awareness/recognition a → revelation, which includes recognising God the Father, Son and Holy Spirit

Stoicism, ancient (ca 300 BC) regressive philosophy concerned with Virtue ethics among other things

subjective atonement/redemption, different to → objective atonement/redemption, a concept of Christ's death whereby the effects are visible in people without anything having changed objectively in the world

T

Thomas Aquinas, (1225–1274), medieval theologian, was greatly influenced by Aristotle's philosophy intensively. Extremely influential from the Middle Ages to the present day

Transcendence, existence above and independent of the universe; notion that God is above and beyond the world

Trinity, God's being as a relationship between three persons, Father, Son and Holy Spirit in communion; became church doctrine in Constantinopel in 381

Truth, Goodness and Beauty, the three "transcendentals" of classical philosophy; in Neoplatonism and Idealism they are interchangeable with each other and with being itself

Trust (lat. fiducia), fundamental element of faith

V

Verficationism, view stating that only → verifiable concepts are scientifically valid

Verification, the principle of corroborating statements

Virtues, human character traits

Virtue Ethics, a reflection on human conduct, regarding a person's actions and → Virtues

Voluntarianism, a concept claiming that God's will is a fundamental characteristic

The New Testament

Traditions about Jesus' suffering and death developed apart from the gospel passion narratives. Examining 1 Corinthians, 1 Peter, Hebrews, and the Epistle of Barnabas, this study argues that sories and songs about Jesus' passion took shape in relation to the ritual practices of early christian communities. In this context, the scriptures of Israel – particulary the story of the Israelites' wilderness journey and of Moses' death, the psalms, and other songs of the suffering righteous – contributed to the discourse. The perspective of ritual and performance theory is utilized to examine how ritual and narrative work together to constitute community.

Ellen Bradshaw Aitken
Jesus' Death in Early Christian Memory
The Poetics of the Passion

Novum Testamentum et Orbis Antiquus / Studien zur Umwelt des Neuen Testaments, vol. 53.
2004. 202 pp, cloth
ISBN 3-525-53954-1

Vandenhoeck & Ruprecht/
Academic Press Fribourg

V&R
Vandenhoeck
& Ruprecht

Deuteronomy and Ancient Greek Law

This study aims at an interpretation of the relationship between individual and the society as described in the laws of the book of Deuteronomy and equivalent documents from the ancient Greek world.

Table of Contents

Anselm C. Hagedorn

Between Moses and Plato

Individual and Society in Deuteronomy and Ancient Greek Law

Forschungen zur Religion und Literatur des Alten und Neuen Testaments, vol. 204.
2004. X, 351 pp, cloth
ISBN 3-525-53888-X

V&R
Vandenhoeck
& Ruprecht